Making Isometric Social Real-Time Games with HTML5, CSS3, and Javascript

Mario Andrés Pagella

O'REILLY®

Beijing · Cambridge · Farnham · Köln · Sebastopol · Tokyo

Making Isometric Social Real-Time Games with HTML5, CSS3, and Javascript
by Mario Andrés Pagella

Published by O'Reilly Media, Inc., 1005 Gravenstein Highway North, Sebastopol, CA 95472.

O'Reilly books may be purchased for educational, business, or sales promotional use. Online editions are also available for most titles (*http://my.safaribooksonline.com*). For more information, contact our corporate/institutional sales department: (800) 998-9938 or *corporate@oreilly.com*.

Editor: Simon St. Laurent		**Cover Designer:** Karen Montgomery	
Production Editor: Kristen Borg		**Interior Designer:** David Futato	
Copyeditor: Nancy Kotary		**Illustrator:** Robert Romano	
Proofreader: O'Reilly Production Services			

ISBN: 978-1-449-30475-1

[LSI]

1314293561

To my mother. May God keep you safe until we meet once again.

Table of Contents

Preface

Addictive, frustrating. Fun, boring. Engaging, repetitive. Casual, demanding.

These words may contradict each other, but they express the roller coaster of sentiments felt by real-time strategy games players like me. I remember spending countless hours playing brilliant games such as EA/Maxis's SimCity and SimCity 2000, Chris Sawyer's Transport Tycoon, or Bullfrog Productions' Theme Hospital, wondering why only a few of my friends (usually the geekiest ones) had played them.

Today, I see children and teenagers, grandmothers and soccer moms, and frat boys and computer geeks playing games such as Zynga's FarmVille or CityVille, Playdom's Social City, or Playfish's MyEmpire for hours, ignorant of the existence of those games' predecessors: a golden age of isometric real-time games that they'll probably never play.

What changed?

This recent surge of isometric real-time games was caused partly by Zynga's incredible ability to "keep the positive things and get rid of the negative things" in this particular genre of games, and partly by a shift in consumer interests. They took away the frustration of figuring out why no one was "moving to your city" (in the case of SimCity) and replaced it with adding friends to be your growing neighbors. They took advantage of Facebook's social capabilities to change the nature of gaming. They made the boring parts more interactive by letting you not only place the objects, but also build them and manually collect the points they generate. After a while—usually a few weeks—when the game starts to feel repetitive, they present you with quests and make you interact with your friends. Finally, the constructions that you build will remain, generating profits and points even if you are not playing the game. (This concept is usually referred to in the industry as *asynchronous play* or *asynchronous game mechanics*.)

When you eliminate frustration, boredom, and repetition (the three bad aspects of isometric real-time games), you end up with an addictive, fun, engaging, and casual (or demanding, depending on how you want to play it) genre of games that—thanks to its social-related progress requirements—can go viral in a heartbeat. No wonder Zynga's valuation at the time of writing is $10 billion (surpassing Electronic Arts (EA), one of the biggest "traditional" game publishers in the world), or that Playdom was purchased by Disney for 760 million dollars. Coming up with the right values for each variable of the gameplay equation for your own game is extremely hard, but when you manage to get everything right, the very nature of this genre of social games can make it an instant hit.

The interfaces of isometric social real-time games are simple compared with conventional real-time strategy games: a "living" map editor where you can place objects on a matrix of tiles, which we'll usually refer to as "the grid." Depending on the object, which in our case will be buildings, some of them may generate P amount of points every T amount of time. So even when we're not playing the game, buildings will keep generating points.

As the final project in this book, we're going to develop a game called "Tourist Resort" in which users will have to build a resort complex, decorate it with trees, and place various shops. Each shop will generate N amount of profit every T amount of time; this profit will then allow them to buy more buildings.

The Rise of HTML5

While social isometric game systems were improving, the technologies available to build them were also changing.

For many years, the tools available to develop rich and highly interactive online games that can run within web browsers remained the same; Virtual Reality Modeling Language (VRML), Java Applets, Macromedia Shockwave, Adobe Flash, Microsoft Silverlight, Unity3D, and others all meant using third-party and proprietary solutions, and if users wanted to use those applications, they had to download and install browser add-ons. Even worse was that developers also had to pay for really expensive IDEs (integrated development environments) to develop them.

Web technologies such as HTML, CSS, and JavaScript could not provide users with the same quality end-user experience that could be achieved with other tools such as Adobe Flash. Browsers—particularly with JavaScript—were slow; they lacked support for native video, audio, and local storage; and some of them, such as Internet Explorer, neither supported transparencies in PNG images nor provided developers with tools to perform even basic bit-lock image transfers. They weren't ready for anything but the simplest of games.

Thankfully, as time went by, most major web browsers started to implement the latest version of the HTML and CSS standards: HTML5 and CSS3. At the same time, they greatly improved the runtime performance of JavaScript applications. Nowadays, the most recent versions of modern browsers such as Mozilla Firefox, Apple Safari, Google Chrome, Opera, and Microsoft Internet Explorer 9—as well as the browsers included in smart devices such as the iPhone, Blackberry phones, and WebOS-based and Android-based phones—have already implemented most of the technologies that we need in order to develop a full-featured video game.

What You Need to Know

This book doesn't provide a definitive guide to HTML5, CSS3, or JavaScript. It assumes that you have at least a basic knowledge of how to work with all of those languages. Instead, throughout the different sections of this book, we discuss how to apply these technologies in the most performance-efficient way so that you can develop and launch a game that works *today* in any smartphone, tablet, or PC with a web browser that supports HTML5.

This book is intended for web developers trying to do game development or for game developers trying to adapt their knowledge to web development.

Our main approach for the development of an isometric social real-time strategy game will be to aim at the lowest common denominator: mobile devices. The rationale for this approach is that if it works on a mobile device at a decent speed, it will also work on more high-end devices such as personal computers.

Code Examples

All of the code and other supporting files for examples in this book are available at *https://github.com/andrespagella/Making-Isometric-Real-time-Games*.

Development and Debugging Tools

Even if you're an experienced developer, a few key tools can be helpful. Although you could implement these examples with a simple text editor (like Notepad or TextEdit) and any HTML5-capable web browser, if you intend to do any serious work, it would be nice to have syntax highlighting, a JavaScript console, a JavaScript debugger, and a web inspector. I strongly recommend using an editor that supports (or that can be extended to support) JavaScript, HTML, and CSS, such as vim or emacs.

The JavaScript Console, JavaScript debugger, and the web inspector are tools that can be used to locate and track problems, routines, or objects. Luckily for us, most modern browsers also include the three of them:

Mozilla Firefox
> Inside the Tools menu, you'll find JavaScript Console and Inspect; I strongly recommend installing Firebug, which is an extension made for advanced web development that also includes a JavaScript debugger and an HTML, CSS, and DOM inspector, along with many other features.

Internet Explorer
> Open the Developer Tools by pressing F12. These include a JavaScript console that allows you to view the page in different "document modes" to see how your site will handle visitors using IE5, IE7, IE8, and so on.

Google Chrome

If you access the View menu (in OSX) or click on the little wrench icon that is usually located right next to the address bar, then go to the Developer menu, you will see JavaScript Tools and JavaScript Console. Both of them are toolsets included in most WebKit-based browsers.

Safari

The Advanced tab of the Preferences includes a checkbox at the bottom for "Show Develop menu in menu bar." Alternately, in OS X, you can enable the Develop menu by opening a Terminal window and typing `defaults write com.apple.Safari IncludeDebugMenu 1`. Another approach is to edit the *Preferences.plist* file and add the following line before the `</dict>` and `</plist>` XML closing tags: `<key>IncludeDebugMenu</key><true/>`. In OS X, the *Preferences.plist* file is usually located in one of the following directories, depending on the version of your operating system:

- *C:\Documents and Settings\%USER%\Application Data\Apple Computer\Safari*, where *%USER%* is your account.
- *C:\Users\%USER%\AppData\Roaming\Apple Computer\Safari*, where *%USER%* is your account.

In Microsoft Windows, you can edit the Safari shortcut to add `/enableDebugMenu` right next to the *Safari.exe* path.

Opera 10

Opera also includes a great debugging utility and web inspector called Dragonfly. To learn more, refer to the official Opera Dragonfly website: *http://www.opera.com/dragonfly/*.

Notes on Game Design

Game design is one of the most important aspects (if not *the* most important aspect) of game development: no one wants to play a boring game. In this genre of social real-time strategy games, it is very important to engage the user not only by providing a good user experience and fun gameplay, but also by *heavily* integrating the game into the user's social network and experience.

Don't forget that the main appeal of these sort of games—which appear simple at first glance—is to make the users compete with their friends ("I have a bigger/nicer city than yours"). And there's no better and more convincing advertising than recommendations from your own circle of friends.

You also need to be careful and responsible about how you interact with users' social connections. Getting banned by the social network itself (for example, Facebook) would be a disaster, but even before that happened, the application could get blocked or flagged as spam by players.

Game design is a far broader subject than can be covered here. An excellent book on the blurring of boundaries of game design with web applications is *Gamification by Design* by Gabe Zichermann and Christopher Cunningham (O'Reilly).

Conventions Used in This Book

The following typographical conventions are used in this book:

Italic

> Indicates new terms, URLs, email addresses, filenames, and file extensions.

`Constant width`

> Used for program listings, as well as within paragraphs to refer to program elements such as variable or function names, databases, data types, environment variables, statements, and keywords.

`Constant width bold`

> Shows commands or other text that should be typed literally by the user.

`Constant width italic`

> Shows text that should be replaced with user-supplied values or by values determined by context.

 This icon signifies a tip, suggestion, or general note.

 This icon indicates a warning or caution.

Using Code Examples

This book is here to help you get your job done. In general, you may use the code in this book in your programs and documentation. You do not need to contact us for permission unless you're reproducing a significant portion of the code. For example, writing a program that uses several chunks of code from this book does not require permission. Selling or distributing a CD-ROM of examples from O'Reilly books does require permission. Answering a question by citing this book and quoting example code does not require permission. Incorporating a significant amount of example code from this book into your product's documentation does require permission.

We appreciate, but do not require, attribution. An attribution usually includes the title, author, publisher, and ISBN. For example: *"Making Isometric Social Real-Time Games with HTML5, CSS3, and Javascript* by Mario Andrés Pagella (O'Reilly). Copyright 2011 Mario Andrés Pagella, 978-1-449-30475-1."

If you feel your use of code examples falls outside fair use or the permission given above, feel free to contact us at *permissions@oreilly.com*.

Safari® Books Online

Safari Books Online is an on-demand digital library that lets you easily search over 7,500 technology and creative reference books and videos to find the answers you need quickly.

With a subscription, you can read any page and watch any video from our library online. Read books on your cell phone and mobile devices. Access new titles before they are available for print, and get exclusive access to manuscripts in development and post feedback for the authors. Copy and paste code samples, organize your favorites, download chapters, bookmark key sections, create notes, print out pages, and benefit from tons of other time-saving features.

O'Reilly Media has uploaded this book to the Safari Books Online service. To have full digital access to this book and others on similar topics from O'Reilly and other publishers, sign up for free at *http://my.safaribooksonline.com*.

How to Contact Us

Please address comments and questions concerning this book to the publisher:

O'Reilly Media, Inc.
1005 Gravenstein Highway North
Sebastopol, CA 95472
800-998-9938 (in the United States or Canada)
707-829-0515 (international or local)
707-829-0104 (fax)

We have a web page for this book, where we list errata, examples, and any additional information. You can access this page at:

http://oreilly.com/catalog/9781449304751

To comment or ask technical questions about this book, send email to:

bookquestions@oreilly.com

For more information about our books, courses, conferences, and news, see our website at *http://www.oreilly.com*.

Find us on Facebook: *http://facebook.com/oreilly*

Follow us on Twitter: *http://twitter.com/oreillymedia*

Watch us on YouTube: *http://www.youtube.com/oreillymedia*

Acknowledgments

Thank you to my fiancée Regina, my father Rubén, my family, my closest friends, and my colleagues. To everyone at Minor Studios, especially CEO Martín Repetto and Xavier Amado. I'd also like to thank Simon St.Laurent, my incredibly helpful editor; Shelley Powers, for her very insightful technical review; and everyone else at O'Reilly who made this possible.

CHAPTER 1

Graphics Foundations: Canvas and Sprites

HTML5's canvas element makes it much easier to create complex graphic games, offering far more flexibility and speed than older approaches that relied on moving images around with the Document Object Model (DOM). Canvas lets you draw on an area of the screen directly with JavaScript, letting you apply traditional game graphics approaches in a web context. Though it's a recent addition to the HTML universe, canvas is widely supported on newer desktop *and* mobile browsers.

Working with the canvas Object

The canvas element allows us to define an extremely fast drawable region on the screen that can be controlled using JavaScript with pixel-level accuracy. However, canvas works in *immediate mode*. Unlike Scalable Vector Graphics (SVG, not covered in this book), the calls that we make to the HTML5 Canvas API draw the graphics directly in the canvas, without holding any reference to them once they are displayed. If we want to move our graphics 10 pixels to the right, we need to clear the display and redraw them using the new coordinates. Later on, we discuss a technique called "adaptive tile refresh" that avoids having to clear the whole display just to modify a small part of the canvas.

You can look at the canvas object as if it were a piece of paper; you have many crayons (among other tools) that you can use to draw things on it. So if, for example, you want to draw a red line, grab the red crayon and draw the line. If you want to draw a green line, grab the green crayon. Same thing goes for your drawing "style." If you want to draw a 45° line that goes from the top left to the bottom right, you can either draw it without moving the paper at all, or tilt the paper 45° to the right and draw a straight line from the top to the bottom. (Obviously, the first approach is more efficient.)

Accessing the HTML5 Canvas API is pretty easy. First, add the new HTML5 `canvas` tag to your page and then assign an `id` attribute to it:

```
<canvas id="game" width="100" height="100">
    Your browser doesn't include support for the canvas tag.
</canvas>
```

The text inside the `canvas` tag will be shown to the browsers that do not support the object. Later, you will learn how to discover and handle those sorts of incompatibilities more efficiently using a JavaScript library called Modernizr.

 You need to specify the `width` and `height` attributes inside the `canvas` tag. Even though you can force `canvas` to a certain width and height with CSS, when you reference the object using JavaScript, it will return the default size (300×150 pixels), completely overriding any values that you may have assigned via CSS. However, you *can* modify the width and height of an HTML Canvas object dynamically in JavaScript.

In order to start using the HTML5 Canvas API, we just need to reference the `canvas` tag by using its `id` attribute value (`myCanvas`), which will allow us to get a reference to the 2D drawing context. (The "3D Context" is WebGL, which is not covered in this book.)

```
window.onload = function () {
  var canvas = document.getElementById('game');
  var c = canvas.getContext('2d');
}
```

Alternatively, you can create an HTML5 Canvas object dynamically:

```
window.onload = function () {
  var canvas = document.createElement('canvas');
  var c = canvas.getContext('2d');
}
```

In the previous example code, the reference to the 2D drawing context is stored in the `c` variable (in many other examples, this variable might be called `ctx`). All further calls to the canvas API will be done through this variable. As an initial example, we're going to work on the very first thing that users will see when they load our game: *The Title Screen*. Later on, we're going to extend it to support the preloading of resources such as images or sounds.

Our title screen, which will be displayed throughout the entire browser window, will consist of an image showing the logo of our game and a text below it with the phrase "Click or tap the screen to start the game." When you click on the browser window, the title screen will smoothly fade to white.

In order to get started with this, we need to add the basic HTML code that will support the game. In most cases, the page is going to look like a conventional HTML5 page:

```
<!DOCTYPE html>
<html lang="en">
  <head>
    <meta charset="UTF-8" />
    <title>Example 1 - Title Screen</title>

    <script>
      // Javascript code goes here
    </script>
    <style type="text/css" media="screen">
      html { height: 100%; overflow: hidden }
     body {
         margin: 0px;
         padding: 0px;
         height: 100%;
       }
    </style>

  </head>
  <body>
    <canvas id="game" width="100" height="100">
      Your browser doesn't include support for the canvas tag.
    </canvas>
  </body>
</html>
```

The small CSS block in the previous code allows us to force the page to be 100 percent of the height of the window, and overflow: hidden prevents vertical and horizontal scrollbars from showing up if we exceed the visible area on the screen.

Now that our page template is complete, we can start using the HTML5 Canvas API by adding the following JavaScript code inside the <script> tag of our page:

```
window.onload = function () {
  var canvas = document.getElementById('game');

  // Force canvas to dynamically change its size to
  // the same width/height as the browser window
  canvas.width = document.body.clientWidth;
  canvas.height = document.body.clientHeight;

  var c = canvas.getContext('2d');

  // Fill the screen with a black background
  c.fillStyle = '#000000';
  c.fillRect (0, 0, canvas.width, canvas.height);

  var phrase = "Click or tap the screen to start the game";
  c.font = 'bold 16px Arial, sans-serif';
  c.fillStyle = '#FFFFFF';
  c.fillText (phrase, 10, 30);
}
```

Let's go through this code step by step.

When we added the `canvas` tag to the HTML code, we defined the `height` and the `width` attributes with the value `100`, meaning that the canvas should be 100 pixels tall and 100 pixels wide. However, we wanted our title screen to be as tall and wide as the browser window, which is why we needed to override those two values dynamically by using `document.body.clientWidth` to indicate the width and `document.body.client Height` to indicate the height.

After we get a reference to the 2D context, we make a call to an HTML5 Canvas API function called `fillStyle()`. At the beginning of this chapter, we made a comparison of the canvas to a piece of paper with crayons of different colors; this is the same scenario. What the `fillStyle()` call is doing is to set the color to black, and after that it draws a filled rectangle starting at position (0,0) and ending at position (`can vas.width`, `canvas.height`), thus covering the entire browser window. (Remember that we set a new size for the `canvas` object in the last step.)

Then it sets the phrase that we're going to use, selects a font family (in this case, Arial with a fallback to sans-serif, which works exactly as in CSS) and size, and changes the color again, this time to white. The `fillText()` call prints the phrase on the position 10, 30 (10 pixels starting on the left, 30 pixels starting on the top).

Figure 1-1 shows the result of that code.

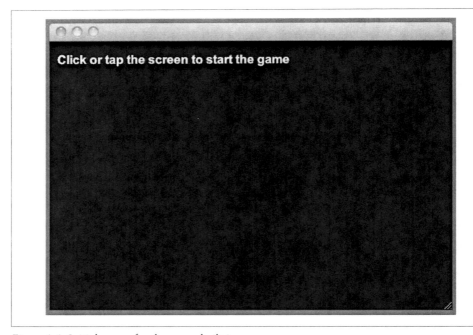

Figure 1-1. Initial screen for the game; built-in canvas

The HTML5 Canvas API also includes a very useful method called measure Text(*phrase*) that returns the width (in pixels) of the *phrase* parameter. We also need to be careful to measure the text *after* we set the size of the font, not before. Using measureText(), we can center the text on the screen:

```
var phrase = "Click or tap the screen to start the game";
c.font = 'bold 16px Arial, sans-serif';
var mt = c.measureText(phrase);
var xcoord = (canvas.width / 2) - (mt.width / 2);
c.fillStyle = '#FFFFFF';
c.fillText (phrase, xcoord, 30);
```

So far we have painted the canvas black, and we specified only hexadecimal color values as the parameter for the fillStyle() method. Other styles supported by canvas are:

- Color keywords such as 'red' or 'black'
- RGB values in the format rgb(*Red, Green, Blue)*
- RGBA values in the format rgba(*Red, Green, Blue, Alpha*), where the *Alpha* parameter (the transparency) goes from 0.0 to 1.0
- HSL values in the format hsl(*Percentage, Percentage, Percentage*)
- HSLA values in the format hsla(*Percentage, Percentage, Percentage, Alpha*)

If solid colors aren't enough for you, canvas also makes it possible to:

- Display a linear gradient by using createLinearGradient()
- Display a radial gradient by using createRadialGradient()
- Display an image/canvas or video pattern by using createPattern()

In order to change the example so that it displays a nice blue gradient instead of a black background, we can use the following code:

```
var grd = c.createLinearGradient(0, 0, canvas.width, canvas.height);
grd.addColorStop(0, '#ceefff');
grd.addColorStop(1, '#52bcff');

c.fillStyle = grd;
c.fillRect(0, 0, canvas.width, canvas.height);
```

Displaying images on the canvas is just as easy as displaying text using the *draw Image()* method:

```
var img = new Image();
img.src = 'image.png';
c.drawImage(img, 0, 0, img.width, img.height);
```

 In order to use the img.width and img.height attributes, the img.ready State property must be equal to COMPLETE. In the final game implementation, we'll take care of this with a resource loader The resource loader can be found within the *game.js* folder of the code repository (the file is called *resourceLoader.js*).

The `drawImage()` method of the HTML5 Canvas API has three different implementations. Although we'll be covering most of them in the following sections, a more detailed document explaining each implementation can be found here: *http://www.w3.org/TR/2dcontext/#dom-context-2d-drawimage*.

If we want to make our image twice as big as the original size, we just need to multiply its size by 2 in the following way:

```
var img = new Image();
img.src = 'image.png';
c.drawImage(img, 0, 0, img.width * 2, img.height * 2);
```

In our case, we're going to use a file provided in the official code repository within the *img* directory, called *logo.png*. We're also going to present the image so that it fills 50% of the browser window while maintaining its width/height aspect ratio so that it can be displayed gracefully in mobile phones or tablets as well as conventional desktop computers.

To present the title screen, make a function called `showIntro()` that displays the blue gradient, the image, and the text:

```
function showIntro () {
    var phrase = "Click or tap the screen to start the game";

    // Clear the canvas
    c.clearRect (0, 0, canvas.width, canvas.height);

    // Make a nice blue gradient
    var grd = c.createLinearGradient(0, canvas.height, canvas.width, 0);
    grd.addColorStop(0, '#ceefff');
    grd.addColorStop(1, '#52bcff');

    c.fillStyle = grd;
    c.fillRect(0, 0, canvas.width, canvas.height);

    var logoImg = new Image();
    logoImg.src = '../img/logo.png';

    // Store the original width value so that we can keep
    // the same width/height ratio later
    var originalWidth = logoImg.width;

    // Compute the new width and height values
    logoImg.width = Math.round((50 * document.body.clientWidth) / 100);
    logoImg.height = Math.round((logoImg.width * logoImg.height) / originalWidth);

    // Create an small utility object
    var logo = {
        img: logoImg,
        x: (canvas.width/2) - (logoImg.width/2),
        y: (canvas.height/2) - (logoImg.height/2)
    }
```

```
    // Present the image
    c.drawImage(logo.img, logo.x, logo.y, logo.img.width, logo.img.height);

    // Change the color to black
    c.fillStyle = '#000000';
    c.font = 'bold 16px Arial, sans-serif';

    var textSize = c.measureText (phrase);
    var xCoord = (canvas.width / 2) - (textSize.width / 2);

    c.fillText (phrase, xCoord, (logo.y + logo.img.height) + 50);
}
```

Calling the showIntro() function will display the image shown in Figure 1-2.

Figure 1-2. Screenshot of the Example 1-1 title screen

Now that our main "title screen" is ready, let's work on the routine that makes the screen fade to white. To accomplish this, we're going to use a function called fadeTo White() that will call itself every 30 milliseconds until the entire screen is covered in white.

If we want to paint an area with a specific opacity, there are two approaches that we can use:

• Specify a fill color in RGBA or HSLA
• Change the globalAlpha parameter in the 2D Context to a value between 0.0 (transparent) and 1.0 (solid)

The globalAlpha parameter (which is the approach that we'll be using) allows us to specify with how much opacity elements should be displayed on the screen from that point on. Once we set an opacity of, for example, 0.5, all other fillRects, fillTexts, drawImages, and similar calls will be 50% translucent.

The fadeToWhite() function will look like this:

```
function fadeToWhite(alphaVal) {
  // If the function hasn't received any parameters, start with 0.02
  var alphaVal = (alphaVal == undefined) ? 0.02 : parseFloat(alphaVal) + 0.02;

  // Set the color to white
  c.fillStyle = '#FFFFFF';
  // Set the Global Alpha
  c.globalAlpha = alphaVal;

  // Make a rectangle as big as the canvas
  c.fillRect(0, 0, canvas.width, canvas.height);

  if (alphaVal < 1.0) {
    setTimeout(function() {
      fadeToWhite(alphaVal);
    }, 30);
  }
}
```

All that is left for us to do now is to attach the click and resize events. The complete Example 1-1, shown here, can also be downloaded from the official repository, where you'll be able to find it as *ex1-titlescreen.html* inside the *examples* folder. For the sake of brevity, some functions such as fadeToWhite() and showIntro() are empty, as they were just shown.

Example 1-1. The opening screen

```
<!DOCTYPE html>
<html lang="en">
  <head>
    <meta charset="UTF-8" />
    <title>Example 1 - Title Screen</title>

    <script>
      window.onload = function () {
        var canvas = document.getElementById('myCanvas');
        var c = canvas.getContext('2d');

        var State = {
          _current: 0,
          INTRO: 0,
          LOADING: 1,
          LOADED: 2
        }

        window.addEventListener('click', handleClick, false);
        window.addEventListener('resize', doResize, false);

        doResize();

        function handleClick() {
          State._current = State.LOADING;
          fadeToWhite();
```

```
      }

      function doResize() {
        canvas.width = document.body.clientWidth;
        canvas.height = document.body.clientHeight;

        switch (State._current) {
          case State.INTRO:
              showIntro ();
              break;
        }
      }

      function fadeToWhite(alphaVal) {
        // ...
      }

      function showIntro () {
        // ...
      }
    }
  </script>
  <style type="text/css" media="screen">
    html { height: 100%; overflow: hidden }
    body {
      margin: 0px;
      padding: 0px;
      height: 100%;
    }
  </style>

</head>
<body>
  <canvas id="myCanvas" width="100" height="100">
    Your browser doesn't include support for the canvas tag.
  </canvas>
</body>
</html>
```

Although in this case, the animation being performed (the fade to white) is not too complex, if you run more complex animation examples on a mobile device, you will probably notice small interruptions in the animation, an effect called "frame skipping."

Creating Smooth Animations

In any sort of game development, it's critical to make the most efficient use of resources. However quickly canvas may be able to draw elements on the screen, we still need to clear or redraw a large area several times per second; although the game perhaps won't feel "jerky" on personal computers, mobile devices such as cell phones or tablets could struggle to keep up, which would completely ruin the game experience for our players. (Later in this chapter, you will learn how to dramatically improve performance.)

The enormous variety of devices that will be able to play our game means that if we need to present a simple animation, some devices might be able to show them at 90 frames per second (FPS) while others could be doing only 15 FPS.

Example 1-2 shows a simple test that can tell us approximately how capable a device is.

Example 1-2. Testing device capabilities with canvas

```html
<!DOCTYPE html>
<html lang="en">
  <head>
    <meta charset="UTF-8" />
    <title>Canvas Example 2 (FPS Count)</title>

    <script>
      window.onload = function () {
        var canvas = document.getElementById('myCanvas');
        var c = canvas.getContext('2d');

        var fpsArray = [];
        var fpsCount = 0;
        var stopAt = 10;
        var fps = 0;
        var startTime = 0;

        var date = new Date();
        startTime = Math.round(date.getTime() / 1000);

        c.font = '20px _sans';

        draw(startTime);

        function draw (timeStamp) {
          var date = new Date();
          ts = Math.round(date.getTime() / 1000);

          if (timeStamp !== ts) {
            fps = fpsCount;
            fpsCount = 0;
            fpsArray.push(fps);
          } else {
            fpsCount++;
          }

          c.fillStyle = '#000000';
          c.fillRect (0, 0, canvas.width, canvas.height);

          c.fillStyle = '#FFFFFF';
          c.fillText ("TS: " + timeStamp, 10, 20);
          c.fillText ("FPS: " + fps, 10, 40);

          if (timeStamp <= (startTime + stopAt)) {
            setTimeout(function() {
                draw(ts);
            }, 1);
```

```
      } else {
        showResults(c, canvas);
      }
    }

  function showResults() {
    var mean = 0;
    var sum = 0;

    c.fillStyle = '#FFFFFF';
    c.fillRect (0, 0, canvas.width, canvas.height);

    // sort the samples
    for (var i = 0; i < fpsArray.length; i++) {
      for (var j = fpsArray.length - 1; j > i; j--) {
          if (fpsArray[j - 1] > fpsArray[j]) {
            fpsArray[j - 1] = fpsArray[j];
        }
      }
    }

    // discard the first value, which is usually very low
    fpsArray = fpsArray.slice (1, fpsArray.length);

    for (var i = 0; i < fpsArray.length; i++) {
      sum = sum + fpsArray[i];
    }

    mean = sum / fpsArray.length;

    c.fillStyle = '#000000';
    c.fillText ("MIN: " + fpsArray[0], 10, 20);
    c.fillText ("MAX: " + fpsArray[fpsArray.length - 1], 10, 40);
    c.fillText ("MEAN: " + (Math.round(mean * 10) / 10), 10, 60);
    }
  }
  </script>

</head>
<body>
  <canvas id="myCanvas" width="160" height="70" style="border: 1px solid black;">
    Your browser doesn't include support for the canvas tag.
  </canvas>
</body>
</html>
```

Example 1-2 repaints the same canvas object as many times as it can per second for 10 seconds, keeping track of the frame rate. You will notice that in this particular example (at the time of writing this book), Google Chrome and Opera have almost four times better performance than Firefox, Safari, or IE9. Chrome or Opera aren't that much faster than the rest, but there is an artificial limitation in the setTimeout() and setInterval() functions. In most browsers, 10 ms (milliseconds) is the minimum value, but in Chrome and Opera, it is 4 ms. These artificial limitations are set to prevent the browser from locking up and are defined in the W3C Working Draft (*http://www.w3 .org/TR/html5/timers.html*).

A more "browser-friendly" approach is to use the `requestAnimFrame` function (because the HTML5 spec is still being developed, each browser engine has given this function its own name). Using `requestAnimFrame` allows the browser to decide when it is the best time to show the next frame. For example, if we minimize the browser window and nothing else depends on the call to `requestAnimFrame`, the browser could decide to stop the animation until we restore the window to a visible state.

Inside the *examples* folder in the code repository of this book, you will find instructions on how to perform the same task (calculating FPS) using both approaches (*ex2-fps-requestAnimationFrame.html* and *ex2-fps-setTimeout.html*). You can track the progress of timing control for script-based animations in the W3C Editor's Draft (see *http://webstuff.nfshost.com/anim-timing/Overview.html* and *http://www.w3.org/TR/ 2011/WD-animation-timing-20110602/*). The *ex2-fps-requestAnimationFrame.html* file implements a *shim*, a routine that checks whether a given function is implemented by the web browser—and if it isn't, falls back to another, developed by Paul Irish (*http: //paulirish.com*). It checks whether the browser currently supports `requestAnim Frame()` and falls back to `setTimeout()` if it doesn't.

In the following examples and throughout our game, we will stick with the `setTime out()` approach, as it gives us more fine-grained control over when to call the next frame. For example, instead of calling the `setTimeout()` function every 1 or 10 ms, we might decide that it'd be more efficient to call it every 500 or 2000 ms. Although at the time of writing this book, it is not completely supported across all browsers, in the future the final `requestAnimFrame()` function will allow us to specify a time parameter.

`requestAnimFrame` is capped at 60 FPS.

As we have seen so far, depending on the capabilities and the performance of the device (among other factors), we will get a higher or lower FPS—which means that if we base our animations by the number of frames, the animations will be played faster on some devices than on others.

Those familiar with PCs in the 1980s may remember the "turbo" button, which allowed you to change the clock speed of the processor. In the past, many games and applications were developed to run at a specific clock speed, so as computers got faster, all the variables in those games, including the animations, got faster as well, leading to hilarious results. The button allowed us to "slow down" the computer to support old applications such as games.

To prevent this variance, we are going to use a "time-based" approach for animations, in which it doesn't matter how many FPSs our device can process but will rather allow us to specify that an animation should be played within a specific time value, ignoring how many frames that animation actually has.

Working with Sprites

In order to demonstrate this idea, we're going to use an Sprite class, which loads images from a *sprite sheet*. Sprites are individual game textures that may have one (static) or multiple frames (animated). Usually, in order to optimize load and memory lookup times, most of the images in our game will be placed in a single (and large) image file called a sprite sheet. The sprite sheet that we will be using can be seen in Figure 1-3.

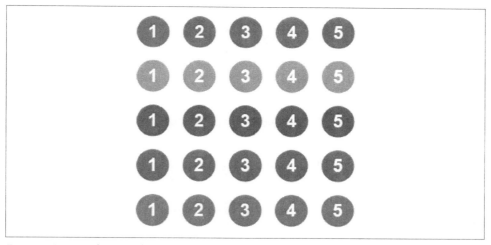

Figure 1-3. A simple sprite sheet

The sprite sheet contains 25 graphics grouped in 5 groups of 5 graphics each, which means that in this case it contains 5 different animations. What we are going to do is to define that the first animation should last 5 seconds; the second should last 2.5 seconds; the third should last 1.6 seconds; the fourth should last 1.25 seconds; and the final one should last only 1 second. Example 1-3 shows how to implement this concept.

Example 1-3. Creating a simple animation with a sprite sheet

```
<!DOCTYPE html>
<html lang="en">
  <head>
    <meta charset="UTF-8" />
    <title>Canvas Example 3 (Sprite Animations)</title>
```

```
<script charset="utf-8" src="sprite.js"></script>
<script>
  var fpsCount = 0;
  var fps = 0;
  var startTime = 0;

  var Timer = function() {
    this.date = new Date();
  }

  Timer.prototype.update = function() {
    var d = new Date();
    this.date = d;
  }

  Timer.prototype.getMilliseconds = function() {
    return this.date.getTime();
  }

  Timer.prototype.getSeconds = function() {
    return Math.round(this.date.getTime() / 1000);
  }

  window.onload = function() {
    var canvas = document.getElementById('myCanvas');
    var c = canvas.getContext('2d');

    // Initialize our sprites
    var spritesheet = '../img/sprite1.png';

    var gray = new Sprite(spritesheet, 60, 60, 0, 0, 5, 5000);
    var yellow = new Sprite(spritesheet, 60, 60, 0, 60, 5, 2500);
    var red = new Sprite(spritesheet, 60, 60, 0, 120, 5, 1666);
    var blue = new Sprite(spritesheet, 60, 60, 0, 180, 5, 1250);
    var green = new Sprite(spritesheet, 60, 60, 0, 240, 5, 1000);

    var timer = new Timer();

    c.font = '14px _sans';

    var startTime = timer.getSeconds();
    draw(startTime);

    function draw (timeStamp) {
      timer.update();

      if (timeStamp !== timer.getSeconds()) {
        fps = fpsCount;
        fpsCount = 0;
      } else {
        fpsCount++;
      }

      c.fillStyle = '#FFFFFF';
      c.fillRect (0, 0, canvas.width, canvas.height);
```

```
        c.fillStyle = '#000000';

        gray.setPosition(40, 60);
        gray.animate(c, timer);
        gray.draw(c);

        yellow.setPosition(80, 100);
        yellow.animate(c, timer);
        yellow.draw(c);

        red.setPosition(120, 140);
        red.animate(c, timer);
        red.draw(c);

        blue.setPosition(160, 180);
        blue.animate(c, timer);
        blue.draw(c);

        green.setPosition(200, 220);
        green.animate(c, timer);
        green.draw(c);

        c.fillText ("Elapsed Time: " + (timeStamp - startTime) + " Seconds", 10, 20);
        c.fillText ("FPS: " + fps, 10, 40);

        setTimeout(function() {
          draw(timer.getSeconds());
        }, 1);
      }
    }
  </script>

  </head>
  <body>
    <canvas id="myCanvas" width="300" height="300" style="border: 1px solid black;">
      Your browser doesn't include support for the canvas tag.
    </canvas>
  </body>
</html>
```

sprite.js, which we'll be using in this and other sections, looks like this:

```
var Sprite = function(src, width, height, offsetX, offsetY, frames, duration) {
    this.spritesheet = null;
    this.offsetX = 0;
    this.offsetY = 0;
    this.width = width;
    this.height = height;
    this.frames = 1;
    this.currentFrame = 0;
    this.duration = 1;
    this.posX = 0;
    this.posY = 0;
    this.shown = true;
    this.zoomLevel = 1;
```

```
        this.setSpritesheet(src);
        this.setOffset(offsetX, offsetY);
        this.setFrames(frames);
        this.setDuration(duration);

        var d = new Date();
        if (this.duration > 0 && this.frames > 0) {
            this.ftime = d.getTime() + (this.duration / this.frames);
        } else {
            this.ftime = 0;
        }
    }

    Sprite.prototype.setSpritesheet = function(src) {
        if (src instanceof Image) {
            this.spritesheet = src;
        } else {
            this.spritesheet = new Image();
            this.spritesheet.src = src;
        }
    }

    Sprite.prototype.setPosition = function(x, y) {
        this.posX = x;
        this.posY = y;
    }

    Sprite.prototype.setOffset = function(x, y) {
        this.offsetX = x;
        this.offsetY = y;
    }

    Sprite.prototype.setFrames = function(fcount) {
        this.currentFrame = 0;
        this.frames = fcount;
    }

    Sprite.prototype.setDuration = function(duration) {
        this.duration = duration;
    }

    Sprite.prototype.animate = function(c, t) {
        if (t.getMilliseconds() > this.ftime) {
            this.nextFrame ();
        }

        this.draw(c);
    }

    Sprite.prototype.nextFrame = function() {
        if (this.duration > 0) {
            var d = new Date();
```

```
            if (this.duration > 0 && this.frames > 0) {
                this.ftime = d.getTime() + (this.duration / this.frames);
            } else {
                this.ftime = 0;
            }

            this.offsetX = this.width * this.currentFrame;

            if (this.currentFrame === (this.frames - 1)) {
                this.currentFrame = 0;
            } else {
                this.currentFrame++;
            }
        }
    }

    Sprite.prototype.draw = function(c) {
        if (this.shown) {

            c.drawImage(this.spritesheet,
                        this.offsetX,
                        this.offsetY,
                        this.width,
                        this.height,
                        this.posX,
                        this.posY,
                        this.width * this.zoomLevel,
                        this.height * this.zoomLevel);
        }
    }
```

You'll be able to find an additional example in the code repository named *ex3-sprite-anim-alt.html*. A screenshot of this example can be seen in Figure 1-4.

What's at that Pixel?

Another great feature of the HTML5 Canvas is that it allows us to access, or set, the pixel-level information of an image, giving us the possibility of finding out the RGBA values of a specific pixel inside it. The way to do this is by using the `context.getImage Data()` or `context.putImageData()` methods, which take the following parameters:

```
context.getImageData(x, y, width, height);
```

`getImageData()` returns an object called "ImageData" that contains the following fields:

width *(read-only)*
    The width of the image, expressed in pixels

height *(read-only)*
    The height of the image, expressed in pixels

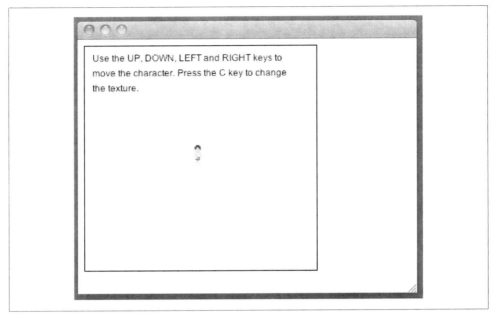

Use the UP, DOWN, LEFT and RIGHT keys to move the character. Press the C key to change the texture.

Figure 1-4. Screenshot of the alternative version of Example 1-3

data

> A `CanvasPixelArray` object (an array) containing all the pixels inside the image, where each pixel is formed by groups of four indexes (R, G, B and A). To access the blue value of the first pixel, call `ImageData.data[2]`. To access the red value of the second pixel, call `ImageData.data[4]`, and so on.

A common iteration going through all the values of an `ImageData.data` array of the whole canvas would look like this:

```
var img = context.getImageData(0, 0, canvas.width, canvas.height);
var idata = img.data; // It's important to save this value
                      // to a new array for performance reasons

for (var i = 0, idatal = idata.length; i < idatal; i += 4) {
  var red = idata[i + 0];
  var green = idata[i + 1];
  var blue = idata[i + 2];
  var alpha = idata[i + 3];
}
```

If instead of accessing image data, you want to insert it into the canvas, you can use:

```
context.putImageData(ImageData.data, x, y);
```

or its alternative implementation:

```
context.putImageData(ImageData.data, x, y, dx, dy, dw, dh);
```

where the parameters would be:

`ImageData.data`
> A `CanvasPixelArray` object (the pixel array)

x
> Origin point of the X axis (upper-left corner) where the `CanvasPixelArray` will be painted

y
> Origin point of the Y axis (upper-left corner) where the `CanvasPixelArray` will be painted

[Optional] dx *("Dirty X")*
> The horizontal value at which to place the `CanvasPixelArray` in the canvas

[Optional] dy *("Dirty Y")*
> The vertical value at which to place the `CanvasPixelArray` in the canvas

[Optional] dw *("Dirty Width")*
> Allows you to specify the width of the `CanvasPixelArray` before being painted onto the canvas (for example, specifying original width/2 would shrink the image horizontally by 50%)

[Optional] dh *("Dirty Height")*
> Allows you to specify the height of the `CanvasPixelArray` before being painted onto the canvas (for example, specifying original height/2 would shrink the image vertically by 50%)

 In order to locally try the following examples in this chapter, you might need to pass on a parameter called `--allow-file-access-from-files` to the Google Chrome, Firefox, or Opera binaries upon startup in order to bypass a security constraint concerning the same-origin policy (each file:// has its own policy).

For more information about this constraint, visit the relevant W3C spec at *http://dev.w3.org/html5/spec/Overview.html#security-with-canvas-elements*.

Safari doesn't have this constraint.

Example 1-4 shows how to apply the `getImageData()` function in a practical context, where we can use it to detect the color of a particular pixel inside an image.

Example 1-4. Detecting pixel color on a canvas

```
<!DOCTYPE html>
<html lang="en">
  <head>
    <meta charset="UTF-8" />
    <title>Canvas Example 4 (Detecting Colors)</title>
```

```
<script>
  window.onload = function () {
    var preview = document.getElementById('preview');
    var r = document.getElementById('r');
    var g = document.getElementById('g');
    var b = document.getElementById('b');
    var a = document.getElementById('a');
    var mx = document.getElementById('mx');
    var my = document.getElementById('my');

    var canvas = document.getElementById('myCanvas');
    canvas.addEventListener('mousemove', move, false);

    var c = canvas.getContext('2d');

    var building = new Image()
    building.src = "../img/cinema.png";

    draw();

    function draw () {
      c.drawImage(building, 0, 0, canvas.width, canvas.height);
    }

    function move (e) {
      mx.innerHTML = e.clientX;
      my.innerHTML = e.clientY;

      var img = c.getImageData(e.clientX, e.clientY, 1, 1);
      var idata = img.data;

      var red = idata[0];
      var green = idata[1];
      var blue = idata[2];
      var alpha = idata[3];

      r.innerHTML = red;
      g.innerHTML = green;
      b.innerHTML = blue;

      a.innerHTML = (alpha > 0) ? alpha : 'Transparent';

        var rgba='rgba(' + red + ', ' + green + ', ' + blue + ', ' + alpha + ')';
      preview.style.backgroundColor =rgba;
    }
  }
</script>

<style type="text/css" media="screen">
  body { margin: 0px; padding: 0px; }

  canvas {
    border: 1px solid black;
    float: left;
  }
```

```
    ul {
      list-style: none;
      margin: 10px 10px 10px 10px;
      padding: 0px;
      float: left;
    }

    ul li { font-weight: bold; }
    ul li span { font-weight: normal; }
    ul li #preview { width: 50px; height: 50px; border: 1px solid black; }
  </style>
</head>
<body>
  <canvas id="myCanvas" width="300" height="300">
    Your browser doesn't include support for the canvas tag.
  </canvas>
  <ul>
    <li><div id="preview"></div></li>
    <li>Red: <span id="r">NULL</span></li>
    <li>Green: <span id="g">NULL</span></li>
    <li>Blue: <span id="b">NULL</span></li>
    <li>Alpha: <span id="a">NULL</span></li>
    <li>Mouse X: <span id="mx">NULL</span></li>
    <li>Mouse Y: <span id="my">NULL</span></li>
  </ul>
</body>
</html>
```

For more information about these and other pixel manipulation functions, access the relevant W3C Working Draft section: *http://www.w3.org/TR/2dcontext/#pixel-manip ulation*.

Dealing with Transparency

Now that you know how to get the color of a particular pixel in the canvas, including its alpha value (the transparency), we can solve a very common problem in web development that previously could be solved only by using very intricate and inefficient hacks (involving the use of JavaScript and CSS to click through the transparent areas of a PNG image, a div, or another element). The problem is that though some areas of the image are transparent, they still act as a solid rectangle, and thus clicking on the transparent areas returns a reference to the original of the image instead of returning a reference to the next solid object below it.

With these tools in our hands, there are many ways to solve this particular problem, but they all mostly consist of either:

• Figuring out the position of the element using DOM functions and iterating through elements until we find a collision with a "solid" pixel

• Keeping track of the positions where we place objects and in which order they are presented, which is the approach used in conventional game development

The first approach can be implemented by using the document.elementFromPoint() DOM function to determine which element was clicked and if it is an image or an object with a background (either a solid color or an image which may or may not have transparent areas), we can use getImageData() to detect whether the selected pixel is transparent. If that's the case, we can select the parent (and if it's not, we can look for siblings). We can keep traversing the DOM until we find a "solid" color and select that element instead of the image. However, this approach can be nonfunctional, impractical, or downright inefficient if:

- There are elements with a large number of siblings or parent nodes
- We are overriding the z-index of parent elements and "going through" the element should select the element below it (which, in this case, would be a child node)

The second approach requires us to do things in a completely different way than most web developers are used to: keeping track of the coordinates of the objects we present on the screen, and upon a click action, do a hit test to see whether the X and Y coordinates of the mouse are inside the area of any given object. The way to do this is to store the position x, position y, width, and height of every element, as well as the order in which they are being presented on the screen. Then, there are many methods that you can use to cycle through all the elements in order to see which one you have clicked on. Having the position x, position y, width, and height for every object that you present allows you to create rectangles that you can later use to test whether the clientX and clientY values returned by a mouse event (such as mousedown, mousemove, mouseup, click, etc.) are inside them. Figure 1-5 shows how we can keep track of all the objects presented on the screen. MX and MY (*Mouse X and Mouse Y*) represent the click coordinates. Then we can check whether the mouse coordinates are inside any of the other objects (in this case, the object being clicked would be #4).

In our case, we're going to eliminate the two downsides of using document.element FromPoint() by combining it with pointer-events: none, a CSS attribute that lets the browser know that the mouse should not interact with an individual element, completely eliminating the need to traverse the DOM or keeping track of every single object in our screen.

Figure 1-6 shows how our page is going to be organized. Clicks made in the transparent areas of the "Smiley" img should go through the image, and we should get a reference to the "Cheese" div, unless, of course, we click through the transparent areas of the Smiley, and a hole of the Cheese, which should return a reference to the HTML document.

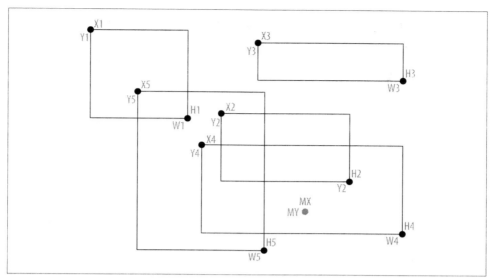

Figure 1-5. Tracking objects on the screen

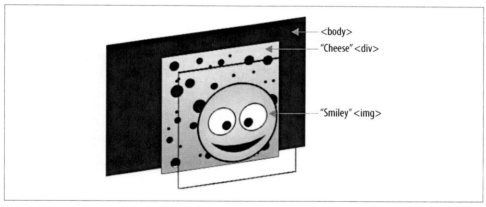

Figure 1-6. A multilayer graphics approach.

To do this, we need to start off by detecting that the page has finished loading:

```
window.onload = function () {
  var MIN_ALPHA_THRESHOLD = 10;

  var canvas = document.getElementById('myCanvas');
  var c = canvas.getContext('2d');

  document.addEventListener('click', detectElement, false);
```

Notice a variable called MIN_ALPHA_THRESHOLD, which specifies how solid something must be (on a scale of 0–255, which is included in the pixel-level data returned by context.getImageData()) so as to not be considered transparent. All the clicks that we make on the document call a function called detectElement().

The idea behind detectElement() is simple; first, we need to detect the object returned by invoking document.elementFromPoint() and test for transparency. If it is transparent, add the object to an array of objects we're going to make "invisible" to pointer events, and try again. Keep doing that until we find a solid object or body, show the result in an alert box, and roll back all the changes:

```
function detectElement (e) {
  var invisibleObjects = new Array();
  var solidPixel = false;
  var obj;

  do {
    obj = document.elementFromPoint(e.clientX, e.clientY);
    if (obj == null || obj.tagName == 'BODY' || obj.tagName == 'HTML') {
      break;
    }
    if (isTransparent(obj, e.clientX, e.clientY)) {
      invisibleObjects.push(obj);
      setObjectEventVisibility(obj, false);
    } else {
      solidPixel = true;
    }
  } while(!solidPixel);

  for (var i = 0; i < invisibleObjects.length; i++) {
    setObjectEventVisibility(invisibleObjects[i], true);
  }

  invisibleObjects = null;

  alert(obj.tagName);
}
```

The setObjectEventVisibility() function makes elements visible or invisible to pointer events by passing a reference to the object, and a boolean parameter indicating whether we want to make objects visible or invisible. All it does is set the value of the pointer Events CSS attribute to either visiblePainted (the default) or none. Other valid values for pointerEvents are visibleFill, visibleStroke, visible, painted, fill, stroke, all, and inherit. You can see the complete list and what each is for in the relevant W3C specification page: *http://www.w3.org/TR/SVG/interact.html#PointerEventsProperty*. Notice that we're going to be assuming that we are not going to be using values for pointerEvents other than visiblePainted or none. Extending the functionality of the function shown here to support all other pointerEvents is left as an exercise to the reader:

```
function setObjectEventVisibility(obj, visible) {
  if (visible) {
    obj.style.pointerEvents = 'visiblePainted';
  } else {
    obj.style.pointerEvents = 'none';
  }
}
```

The function that we're going to be using to detect if an specific coordinate of an image is transparent is called `isPixelTransparent()`. In order to make this function work correctly, we must take into account all the different use-cases in which it will be used. For example, let's say that we have a 300×300-pixel `div`, but as a background we are using a 600×300-pixel image with a horizontal background offset of 300 pixels.

Figure 1-7 shows how the `div` could look (in reality, our background image will be the "cheese" texture) and also shows the complete image being used as its background. Notice that the background of that `div` has a horizontal offset of 300 pixels. If we didn't take that offset into account, clicking on the center of the image would result in a transparent pixel instead of the solid blue one. Another thing to keep in mind (not taken into account in this script) is that in the case of non-`img` elements (such as `divs`), we might be using the CSS3 `background-size` attribute, which allows us to adjust how the background image is presented relative to the `div` that is containing it.

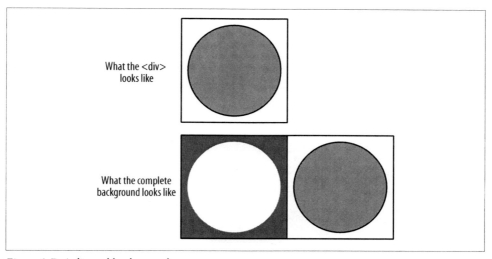

Figure 1-7. A div and background

Therefore, in the case of non-`img` elements, we're going to use the following helper function:

```
function getBackgroundPosition(src, property) {
  property = property.split(' ');
```

```
/**
 * Modifying the code to find out if its inheriting any properties
 * from a parent would be too inefficient. We're going  to be
 * assuming that if the element has 'auto', it means 0
 */
var left = (property[0] != 'auto') ? property[0].substr(0, property[0].length - 2) :
0;
  var top = (property[1] != 'auto') ? property[1].substr(0, property[1].length - 2) : 0;

  return {
    x: left,
    y: top
  };
}
```

For the sake of simplicity, we're going to assume that all background images are not being repeated either horizontally or vertically and that we will be using a single background per element (CSS3 supports multiple backgrounds). However, extending the functions to support multiple backgrounds can be done very easily by loading all of them in an array.

That said, our isPixelTransparent() function is going to look like this:

```
function isPixelTransparent (src, x, y, oWidth, oHeight, offsetX, offsetY) {
    var img = new Image()
    img.src = src;

    // If parameters are not being passed on to this function, use "default" values
    oWidth = (!oWidth) ? img.width : oWidth;
    oHeight = (!oHeight) ? img.height : oHeight;
    offsetX = (!offsetX) ? 0 : offsetX;
    offsetY = (!offsetY) ? 0 : offsetY;

    // 'Reset' the canvas before painting over it again
    c.clearRect(0, 0, 1, 1);

    c.drawImage(img, offsetX - x, offsetY - y, img.width, img.height);

    var idata = c.getImageData(0, 0, 1, 1);
    var data = idata.data;
    var alpha = data[3];

    return (alpha < MIN_ALPHA_THRESHOLD);
}
```

Finally, the isTransparent() function will be in charge of getting the element located at the X and Y coordinates returned by document.elementFromPoint() and figuring out how to interpret it before calling isPixelTransparent().

To do this correctly, we first need to calculate the relative coordinates of the click depending on the position of the object on the screen:

```
function isTransparent(obj, x, y) {
    var robj = obj;
    var rx = robj.x;
```

```
    var ry = robj.y;
    var offset = { x: 0, y: 0 };
    var padding = { x: 0, y: 0 };
    var margin = { x: 0, y: 0 };

    // Calculate the X (left) and Y (top) coordinates relative to the
    // parent until we get to the "top"
    if (robj.offsetParent) {
        rx = 0;
        ry = 0;

        while(robj.offsetParent) {
            rx += robj.offsetLeft;
            ry += robj.offsetTop;
            robj = robj.offsetParent;
        }
    }
```

In addition to the separation between the object and its parent objects, they might also have a padding or a margin defined, so we need to take that possibility into account as well. Figure 1-8 will give you an idea of what a particular scenario might look like.

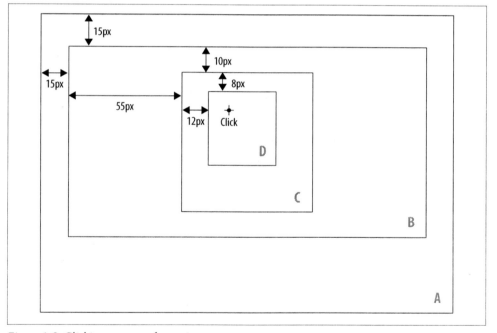

Figure 1-8. Clicking on a set of containers

We have detected a click inside the D container, and we also know that:

```
document.addEventListener('click', detectElement, false);
```

returns coordinates relative to the edges of the window (*container A*). Thus if we want to figure out the X and Y coordinates relative to the D container, we need to cycle through all of D's parent containers (C and B) until we get to the top (A). In this case, that would be:

```
/* Pseudocode */
xCoord = Mouse.x - 12 (C) - 55 (B) - 10 (A)
yCoord = Mouse.y - 8 (C) - 10 (B) - 15 (A)
```

This separation between the container and all of its children could be because:

- We have defined that the children should be positioned using either position: absolute or position: relative, setting a top, left, right, or bottom value(s)
- The container has a padding
- The children have a margin

And so on. However, there are a few "gotchas" in which some of these rules don't apply. For example, if the parent container has defined a padding but its children are using position: absolute, they won't be affected by it.

Usually, to get a CSS attribute, many developers use:

```
document.getElementById('ObjectName').style.property
```

The problem with that approach is that it doesn't take into account CSS attributes defined via a CSS Stylesheet; it can be used only when styles are defined inline. Modern browsers usually support window.getComputedStyle. Here's how to access a property:

```
var cs = document.defaultView.getComputedStyle(obj, null);
paddingLeft = cs.getPropertyValue('padding-left');
```

The name of the computed styles is the same as the CSS attribute that we're trying to access; for example, the left padding would be getPropertyValue('padding-left') and a background image would be getPropertyValue('background-image').

Then we need to figure out what sort of DOM element we're dealing with. Images should be handled in a different way than, say, a div or a td. Elements that do not support background images or "image source" attributes will be considered transparent:

```
switch(obj.tagName) {
  case 'IMG':
    // Handle image source
    break;
  case 'DIV':
  case 'TD':
  case 'P':
  case 'SPAN':
  case 'A':
```

```
    // handle background image or solid color
    break;
  default:
    return true;
    break;
}
```

Conventional img tags are the easiest to handle, as the path to the image is declared in the source attribute:

```
case 'IMG':
  return isPixelTransparent(obj.src, (x - rx), (y - ry), obj.width, obj.height);
  break;
```

However, all other elements require a trickier way to figure out if the object has a solid color or an image background—and if they do, how the image is positioned and presented inside it.

The complete code for this example is *ex5-clickthrough.html* in the *examples* folder of the code repository.

Choosing a Rendering Method for Our Graphics

Just as website download times translate to more or fewer visitors in the statistics (because faster download times reduce visitor dropoff), fluidly rendering graphics and animations on the screen should be one of the most crucial priorities when developing any sort of video game. We'll lose a lot of players if graphics and animations are shaking all the time due to low frame rates. In isometric real-time strategy games, we'll have to keep both things in mind, especially if we want our game to be played on mobile devices as well as desktop computers.

In isometric real-time strategy games, the most basic "objective" of the game is to place buildings on a grid. Each building will generate P amount of points every N number of seconds, which will allow us to buy additional buildings.

Although the most adequate, reliable, and performance-efficient way to draw a grid in a web browser (without using a third-party plugin) depends on the project requirements, there are four possible approaches:

- We can display graphics using WebGL context of the HTML5 Canvas object, which is not covered in this book (see the note following this list).
- We can also present tiles and objects as conventional HTML elements (such as divs or imgs) and position them using the CSS top and left properties. There are two variations of this approach: using isometric-shaped graphics, or rotating and skewing graphics ourselves using CSS3.

- We can deploy a variation of the previous approach, which consists of presenting elements in a similar fashion to the previous method, but using the new CSS3 positioning tools, such as `translateX` and `translateY`—as well as setting `transla teZ(0)`—to force hardware acceleration in Chrome, Safari, and Safari for the iPhone.
- We can use the *2D* context of the HTML5 Canvas object.

Other rendering methods exist but are too inefficient to be used in the context of a video game.

 Although WebGL is the fastest and most efficient method to render graphics on the screen, the reason we're not going to consider it as a reliable method is because, at the time of writing of this book, the WebGL spec hadn't reached version 1.0 and is not supported in the release versions of Internet Explorer 9, Safari for the iPhone, Safari, Android Web Browser, and Opera (Firefox for Android does include support for WebGL, but it needs to be enabled manually in `about:config`). Microsoft has already stated that they won't be supporting WebGL at all due to security concerns (*http://blogs.technet.com/b/srd/archive/ 2011/06/16/webgl-considered-harmful.aspx*). Additionally, WebGL is based on OpenGL ES 2.0—a competing product of DirectX, Microsoft's own graphic library—and also threatens Silverlight (a Rich Internet Application, or RIA, framework for browser-based applications). For more information about the current status of WebGL, refer to the public mailing list on the Khronos Group website: *https://www.khronos.org/ webgl/public-mailing-list/*.

A few weeks before publishing this book, the most efficient way to display the grid was using the third approach, due to the hardware acceleration hack (or feature). The problem with this approach (or the second approach) is that unless we want to keep an enormous number of elements on the DOM tree (one for each tile, plus others for buildings, etc.) when we scroll, we need to constantly add and remove nodes (to display only the elements that we can see, thus keeping the node count low). Adding or removing nodes from the DOM tree triggers a computationally expensive operation on the browser called a *reflow* that allows the layout engine of the browser to compute the geometry of the elements inside the DOM tree. Due to the implementation of hardware acceleration in the 2D and 3D contexts, recent (and future) developments have made and will reinforce the HTML5 Canvas as the most appropriate and efficient graphics rendering method for interactive video games.

The isometric game genre works around building objects on a grid, which is nothing more than a matrix containing two dimensions: one for the "Rows," which we'll sometimes call the "X" axis, and another for the "Columns," which we'll sometimes define as the Y axis. Example 1-5 generates a matrix of 20×50 tiles (20 rows per 50 columns) using this approach.

Example 1-5. Creating a simple grid

```
<!DOCTYPE html>
<html lang="en">
  <head>
    <meta charset="UTF-8" />
    <title>Example 6 (Generating a 20 × 50 grid)</title>
    <script>
      window.onload = function () {
        var tileMap = [];
        var grid = {
          width: 20,
          height: 50
        };

        function initializeGrid() {
          for (var i = 0; i < grid.width; i++) {
            tileMap[i] = [];
            for (var j = 0; j < grid.height; j++) {
              tileMap[i][j] = 0;
            }
          }
        }

        initializeGrid();
      }
    </script>
  </head>
  <body>
  </body>
</html>
```

With the right approach, the size of the grid can be almost unlimited and shouldn't have an impact on performance. We can resort to working with 500×500 or 1,000×1,000 fragments and then, as we are approaching the "beginning" or the "end" of the fragment, we can use a memory paging routine to load/save the fragments, either in the computer hard disk drive—in our case, the WebStorage API—or online in a database. For the sake of simplicity, for our game we will be working with a 250×250 grid (62,500 tiles) and will leave the implementation of a memory paging function as an exercise for the reader.

For the moment, we're going to focus on displaying our grid using squares, and later on, we'll switch to an isometric view.

Let's suppose that we have a really big grid of 6,250,000 tiles (2,500 rows per 2,500 columns) in which each tile has a width and height of 32 pixels and the grid will be displayed in a container that has a resolution of 300×300 pixels. Over the years, when faced with a similar problem (displaying a grid on the screen several times per second), I have seen people doing these sort of things:

```
for (var row = 0; row < grid.length; row++) {
  for (var col = 0; col < grid[row].length; col++) {
    displayTile(row, col);
  }
}
```

This code cycles through every single position on the grid and tries to display the tile without checking whether it is inside the screen. Also, each iteration on both **for** loops (rows and columns) needs to check the size of the grid and grid[row] arrays, so it's terribly inefficient.

Others have been a little bit more generous:

```
for (var row = 0, rowLength = grid.length; row < rowLength; row++) {
  for (var col = 0, colLength = grid[0].length; col < colLength; col++) {
    if (tileIsInsideScreen(row, col)) {
      displayTile(row, col);
    }
  }
}
```

This approach is a *great* performance improvement compared to the previous example. Now the size of the grid array is being stored in a variable (and therefore doesn't need to check the element count on each iteration) and displays the tile only if it can be shown on the screen. However, the main problem remains: it still has to do 6,250,000 iterations. Surely you must be wondering if there's a way to improve on that number. And fortunately for all of us, there is.

The trick consists mainly of iterating through only the elements that you can display by taking into account variables such as the X/Y offset (**scroll**), tile width/height, and display area width/height in the following way:

```
var startRow = Math.floor(scroll.x / tile.width);
var startCol = Math.floor(scroll.y / tile.height);
var rowCount = startRow + Math.floor(canvas.width / tile.width) + 1;
var colCount = startCol + Math.floor(canvas.height / tile.height) + 1;
```

Then you just need to use those variables inside the loops:

```
for (var row = startRow; row < rowCount; row++) {
  for (var col = startCol; col < colCount; col++) {
    displayTile(row, col);
  }
}
```

Example 1-6 demonstrates creating a grid with this approach, and Figure 1-9 compares the results to other approaches.

Example 1-6. Generating a 2500×2500 grid

```
<!DOCTYPE html>
<html lang="en">
  <head>
  <meta charset="UTF-8" />
    <title>Example 7 (Generating a 2500 × 2500 grid)</title>
```

```
<script>
  window.onload = function () {
    var tileMap = [];

    var tile = {
      width: 32,
      height: 32
    }

    var grid = {
      width: 2500,
      height: 2500
    }

    var Keys = {
      UP: 38,
      DOWN: 40,
      LEFT: 37,
      RIGHT: 39
    }

    var scroll = {
      x: 0,
      y: 0
    }

    var canvas = document.getElementById('myCanvas');
    var c = canvas.getContext('2d');

    window.addEventListener('keydown', handleKeyDown, false);

    initializeGrid();
    draw();

    function handleKeyDown(e) {
      switch (e.keyCode) {
        case Keys.UP:
          scroll.y -= ((scroll.y - tile.height) >= 0) ? tile.height : 0;
          break;
        case Keys.DOWN:
          scroll.y += tile.height;
          break;
        case Keys.LEFT:
          scroll.x -= ((scroll.x - tile.width) >= 0) ? tile.width : 0;
          break;
        case Keys.RIGHT:
          scroll.x += tile.width;
          break;
      }

      document.getElementById('scrollx').innerHTML = scroll.x;
      document.getElementById('scrolly').innerHTML = scroll.y;
    }
```

```
      function initializeGrid() {
        for (var i = 0; i < grid.width; i++) {
          tileMap[i] = [];
          for (var j = 0; j < grid.height; j++) {
            if ((i % 2) == 0 && (j % 2) == 0) {
              tileMap[i][j] = 0;
            } else {
              tileMap[i][j] = 1;
            }
          }
        }
      }

      function draw() {
        c.fillStyle = '#FFFFFF';
        c.fillRect (0, 0, canvas.width, canvas.height);
        c.fillStyle = '#000000';

        var startRow = Math.floor(scroll.x / tile.width);
        var startCol = Math.floor(scroll.y / tile.height);
        var rowCount = startRow + Math.floor(canvas.width / tile.width) + 1;
        var colCount = startCol + Math.floor(canvas.height / tile.height) + 1;

        for (var row = startRow; row < rowCount; row++) {
          for (var col = startCol; col < colCount; col++) {
            var tilePositionX = tile.width * row;
            var tilePositionY = tile.height * col;

            tilePositionX -= scroll.x;
            tilePositionY -= scroll.y;

            if (tileMap[row][col] == 0) {
              c.strokeRect(tilePositionX, tilePositionY, tile.width, tile.height);
            } else {
              c.fillRect(tilePositionX, tilePositionY, tile.width, tile.height);
            }
          }
        }

        setTimeout(draw, 1);
      }
    }
  </script>
</head>
<body>
  <canvas id="myCanvas" width="300" height="300"></canvas>
  <br />
  Use the UP, DOWN, LEFT and RIGHT keys to scroll
  <br />
  Scroll X: <span id="scrollx">0</span><br />
  Scroll Y: <span id="scrolly">0</span>
</body>
</html>
```

Although, as Figure 1-9 shows, the difference in performance is *extreme*, there is one more thing that we can optimize. In the previous example, the `initializeGrid()` function took care of filling the `tileMap` matrix with zeros or ones, and storing the 6,250,000 elements in memory. Then, inside the `draw()` loop, we show an empty square if the positions X and Y of the matrix are even and a solid square if they are uneven. We can accomplish the same *without using a matrix at all* by modifying this bit of the `draw()` function:

```
if (tileMap[row][col] == 0) {
  c.strokeRect(tilePositionX, tilePositionY, tile.width, tile.height);
} else {
  c.fillRect(tilePositionX, tilePositionY, tile.width, tile.height);
}
```

```
if ((row % 2) == 0 && (col % 2) == 0) {
  c.strokeRect(tilePositionX, tilePositionY, tile.width, tile.height);
} else {
  c.fillRect(tilePositionX, tilePositionY, tile.width, tile.height);
}
```

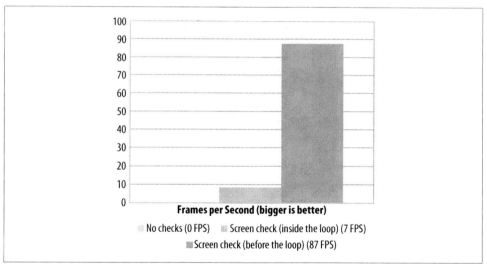

Figure 1-9. Performance optimization results

This small modification allows us to get rid of the grid initialization function, but now our grid is not being imposed with any limits that would allow us to scroll beyond the 2,500×2,500 tiles that we originally planned to use. Although this bug (other developers might call it a feature) could be considered useful for some people, if we want to force the grid to not scroll beyond the 2,500×2,500 boundary, we need to modify another bit of the `draw()` function. We need to change this part of the code:

```
var startRow = Math.floor(scroll.x / tile.width);
var startCol = Math.floor(scroll.y / tile.height);
var rowCount = startRow + Math.floor(canvas.width / tile.width) + 1;
var colCount = startCol + Math.floor(canvas.height / tile.height) + 1;
```

and impose the boundary below, like this:

```
var startRow = Math.floor(scroll.x / tile.width);
var startCol = Math.floor(scroll.y / tile.height);
var rowCount = startRow + Math.floor(canvas.width / tile.width) + 1;
var colCount = startCol + Math.floor(canvas.height / tile.height) + 1;

rowCount = ((startRow + rowCount) > grid.width) ? grid.width : rowCount;
colCount = ((startCol + colCount) > grid.height) ? grid.height : colCount;
```

The entire code for this improved approach can be found on the official code repository as *ex7-grid-canvas-alt.html*. See the result in Figure 1-10.

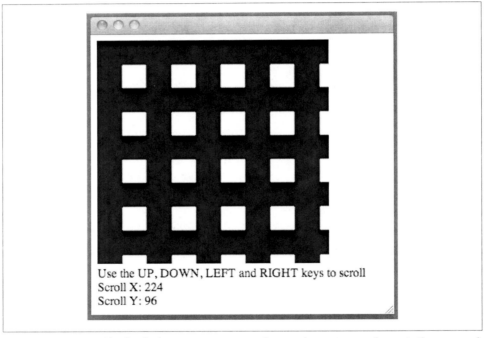

Figure 1-10. Many old-school adventure games using this top-down view employ a similar approach to display their maps

Besides handling the scrolling, we'll probably want to add other ways to interact with the grid, such as changing individual tiles when we click on them.

Translating the pixel coordinates returned by the click event to matrix coordinates in a square grid can be easily accomplished with the following formula:

```
var row = Math.floor(mousePositionX / tileWidth);
var column = Math.floor(mousePositionY / tileHeight);
```

If we need to take into account the scrolling coordinates, we just add them it to the mouse positions like this:

```
var row = Math.floor((mousePositionX + scrollPositionX) / tileWidth);
var column = Math.floor((mousePositionY + scrollPositionY) / tileHeight);
```

Having removed the grid initialization code raises an interesting question: how do we keep track of the elements that we have modified? Luckily for us, we don't need to start arrays indexes on zero, which means that we can do this:

```
tileMap[2423] = [];
tileMap[2423][1803] = 4;
```

Using this approach, we'd store only the elements that we need. Other unset positions in the matrix would just return undefined or null. Example 1-7, *ex8-grid-canvas.html* in the code repository, shows how to implement this idea, with the result shown in Figure 1-11.

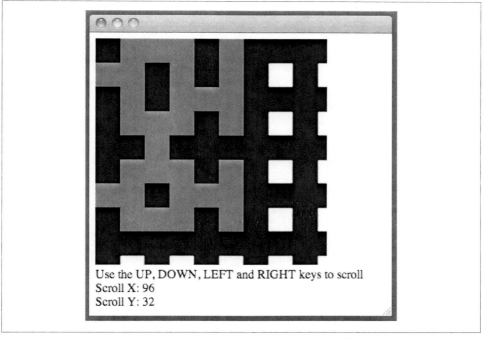

Figure 1-11. Screenshot of Example 1-8; red squares indicate positions that have been clicked by the player

Example 1-7. Storing only the elements we need

```
<!DOCTYPE html>
<html lang="en">
  <head>
    <meta charset="UTF-8" />
    <title>Example 8</title>

    <script>
      window.onload = function () {
        var tileMap = [];

        var tile = {
          width: 32,
          height: 32
        }

        var grid = {
          width: 2500,
          height: 2500
        }

        var Keys = {
          UP: 38,
          DOWN: 40,
          LEFT: 37,
          RIGHT: 39
        }

        var scroll = {
          x: 0,
          y: 0
        }

        var canvas = document.getElementById('myCanvas');
        var c = canvas.getContext('2d');

        canvas.addEventListener('click', handleClick, false);
        window.addEventListener('keydown', handleKeyDown, false);

        draw();

        function handleClick(e) {
          // When a click is detected, translate the mouse
          // coordinates to pixel coordinates
          var row = Math.floor((e.clientX + scroll.x) / tile.width);
          var column = Math.floor((e.clientY + scroll.y) / tile.height);

          if (tileMap[row] == null) {
            tileMap[row] = [];
          }
          tileMap[row][column] = 1;
        }

        function handleKeyDown(e) {
          switch (e.keyCode) {
```

```
    case Keys.UP:
      scroll.y -= ((scroll.y - tile.height) >= 0) ? tile.height : 0;
      break;
    case Keys.DOWN:
      scroll.y += tile.height;
      break;
    case Keys.LEFT:
      scroll.x -= ((scroll.x - tile.width) >= 0) ? tile.width : 0;
      break;
    case Keys.RIGHT:
      scroll.x += tile.width;
      break;
  }

  document.getElementById('scrollx').innerHTML = scroll.x;
  document.getElementById('scrolly').innerHTML = scroll.y;
}

function draw() {

  c.fillStyle = '#FFFFFF';
  c.fillRect (0, 0, canvas.width, canvas.height);
  c.fillStyle = '#000000';

  var startRow = Math.floor(scroll.x / tile.width);
  var startCol = Math.floor(scroll.y / tile.height);
  var rowCount = startRow + Math.floor(canvas.width / tile.width) + 1;
  var colCount = startCol + Math.floor(canvas.height / tile.height) + 1;

  rowCount = ((startRow + rowCount) > grid.width) ? grid.width : rowCount;
  colCount = ((startCol + colCount) > grid.height) ? grid.height : colCount;

  for (var row = startRow; row < rowCount; row++) {
    for (var col = startCol; col < colCount; col++) {
      var tilePositionX = tile.width * row;
      var tilePositionY = tile.height * col;

      tilePositionX -= scroll.x;
      tilePositionY -= scroll.y;

      if (tileMap[row] != null && tileMap[row][col] != null) {
        c.fillStyle = '#CC0000';
        c.fillRect(tilePositionX, tilePositionY, tile.width, tile.height);
        c.fillStyle = '#000000';
      } else {
        if ((row % 2) == 0 && (col % 2) == 0) {
          c.strokeRect(tilePositionX, tilePositionY, tile.width, tile.height);
        } else {
          c.fillRect(tilePositionX, tilePositionY, tile.width, tile.height);
        }
      }
    }
  }

  setTimeout(draw, 1);
```

```
      }
    }
  </script>
</head>
<body>
  <canvas id="myCanvas" width="300" height="300"></canvas>
  <br />
  Use the UP, DOWN, LEFT and RIGHT keys to scroll
  <br />
  Scroll X: <span id="scrollx">0</span><br />
  Scroll Y: <span id="scrolly">0</span>
</body>
</html>
```

So far, all the optimizations that we have made allowed us to increase the performance of our game dramatically, but there is one more thing that we need to take care of before we go on.

The `draw()` loop—the heart and soul of our game, which allows us to display elements on the screen—gets called many times per second, regardless of whether the graphics inside the canvas have changed. On other, more dynamic genres of video games in which we'd find several objects moving on the screen at the same time, this approach would be okay, but in the case of isometric real-time strategy games, most graphics on the screen are usually static, so doing this is a bit unnecessary; we can probably avoid it by calling `draw()` only as needed, instead of calling it many times per second as we are currently doing.

However, also remember that the `draw()` function will render the entire grid after the slightest change, so even calling `draw()` on demand could have a huge performance penalty (see Figure 1-12), especially if we need to animate only a few small objects and leave the rest unchanged.

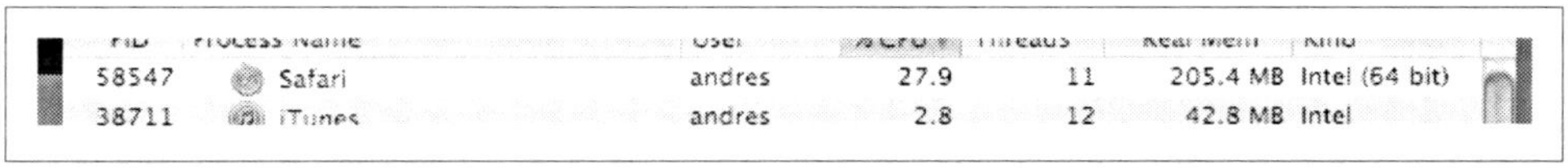

PID	Process Name	User	% CPU	Threads	Real Mem	Kind
58547	Safari	andres	27.9	11	205.4 MB	Intel (64 bit)
38711	iTunes	andres	2.8	12	42.8 MB	Intel

Figure 1-12. CPU usage is at 30% on a PC; on a mobile device, this value would be around 90 or 100%

Back in the early 1990s, while at id Software, John Carmack was working on a game called Commander Keen, the very first side-scroller game released for the PC, when he was faced with a similar problem. To solve it, he invented a technique known as Adaptive Tile Refresh (ATR), in which he redrew only the area that had changed.

In order to implement a similar technique, we need to get rid of the `setTimeout()` in the `draw()` loop and add four parameters to the `draw()` function: `srcX`, `srcY`, `destX`, and `destY`. Calling the `draw()` function without passing any parameters should redraw the entire canvas; passing the `srcX/Y` and `destX/Y` parameters should redraw only the area within that boundary.

Example 1-8 shows how to do this.

Example 1-8. Modified grid using ATR

```
<!DOCTYPE html>
<html lang="en">
  <head>
    <meta charset="UTF-8" />
    <title>Example 9 - Grid modified to work with ATR (Adaptive Tile Refresh)</title>

    <script src="timer.js" charset="utf-8"></script>
    <script src="sprite.js" charset="utf-8"></script>
    <script>
      window.onload = function () {
        var tile = {
          width: 3,
          height: 3
        }

        var grid = {
          width: 100,
          height: 100
        }

        var canvas = document.getElementById('myCanvas');
        var c = canvas.getContext('2d');

        var man1 = new Sprite('../img/char1.png', 32, 32, 0, 96, 4, 200);
        var man2 = new Sprite('../img/char2.png', 32, 32, 0, 224, 6, 400);
        var man3 = new Sprite('../img/char3.png', 32, 32, 0, 128, 4, 600);

        var timer = new Timer();

        // Draw the entire grid
        draw();
        displayAnimatedSprites();

        function displayAnimatedSprites() {
          timer.update();

          man1.setPosition(120, 60);
          man2.setPosition(120, 102);
          man3.setPosition(120, 141);

          // Redraw just the area of the grid being changed
          draw(man1.posX, man1.posY, man1.width, man1.height);
          draw(man2.posX, man2.posY, man2.width, man2.height);
          draw(man3.posX, man3.posY, man3.width, man3.height);

          man1.animate(c, timer);
          man2.animate(c, timer);
          man3.animate(c, timer);

          setTimeout(function() {
            displayAnimatedSprites(timer.getSeconds());
          }, 100);
        }
```

```
function draw(srcX, srcY, destX, destY) {
  srcX = (srcX === undefined) ? 0 : srcX;
  srcY = (srcY === undefined) ? 0 : srcY;
  destX = (destX === undefined) ? canvas.width : destX;
  destY = (destY === undefined) ? canvas.height : destY;

  c.fillStyle = '#FFFFFF';
  c.fillRect (srcX, srcY, destX + 1, destY + 1);
  c.fillStyle = '#000000';

  var startRow = 0;
  var startCol = 0;
  var rowCount = startRow + Math.floor(canvas.width / tile.width) + 1;
  var colCount = startCol + Math.floor(canvas.height / tile.height) + 1;

  rowCount = ((startRow + rowCount) > grid.width) ? grid.width : rowCount;
  colCount = ((startCol + colCount) > grid.height) ? grid.height : colCount;

  for (var row = startRow; row < rowCount; row++) {
    for (var col = startCol; col < colCount; col++) {
      var tilePositionX = tile.width * row;
      var tilePositionY = tile.height * col;

      if (tilePositionX >= srcX && tilePositionY >= srcY &&
        tilePositionX <= (srcX + destX) &&
        tilePositionY <= (srcY + destY)) {

        c.strokeStyle = '#CCCCCC';
        c.strokeRect(tilePositionX, tilePositionY, tile.width, tile.height);
      }
    }
  }
}
    </script>
  </head>
  <body>
    <canvas id="myCanvas" width="300" height="300"></canvas>
  </body>
</html>
```

Figure 1-13 shows that even while running three different animations simultaneously, the CPU usage has gone down dramatically from ~30% to just ~6.5%.

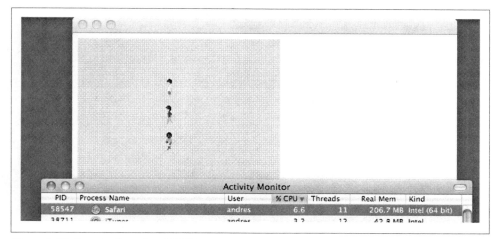

Figure 1-13. Drastically reduced CPU usage

For the sake of simplicity, in this book we allow only one ATR coordinate at a time, but on professional, more complex video games, draw() functions may accept an array with several ATR coordinates, which allows them to refresh many positions with a single call. For example:

```
function  draw(atrArray) {
    for (var i = 0, len = atrArray.length; i < len; i++) {
        if (insideScreen(atrArray[i])) {
            drawGraphic();
        }
    }
}
```

CHAPTER 2

Making It Isometric

Our game, and other isometric games such as Sid Meier's Civilization, Blizzard's Diablo, or Zynga's FarmVille, CityVille, and Café World use a special form of isometric projection (called *dimetric projection*) in which tiles (usually diamonds or hexagons) are displayed in a 2:1 ratio with their height at half their width.

Most game developers choose to display tiles with this specific 2:1 ratio because of a problem unique to raster graphics, which we can understand if we know how computer monitors work. Monitors—whether they are CRT, TFT/LCD, LED, or OLED—display pixels in a grid similar to the one in our game, which allows us to draw perfect vertical or horizontal lines. However, if we need to display a line at an angle than 0° or 90°, things start to get messy. Figure 2-1 shows the resulting problems.

Although the 90°, 45°, and 0° lines have a regular pattern and can be "stitched" with a parallel line perfectly, the 30° line doesn't; it contains gaps instead. However, if we use the 2:1 ratio, we can calculate the inverse tangent (arctangent) of 1/2 to get 26.5650°, producing a result like Figure 2-2.

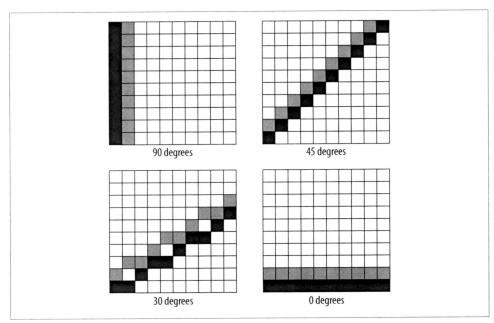

Figure 2-1. Gaps in lines drawn at an angle

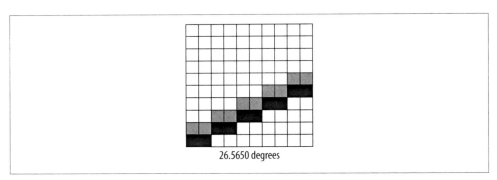

Figure 2-2. A cleaner result at 26.565 degrees

Although so far our grid works only with squares, converting a square texture to an isometric texture can be accomplished easily by using code like that in Example 2-1 to produce a result like the one shown in Figure 2-3.

Example 2-1. Converting squares to an isometric grid

```html
<!DOCTYPE html>
<html lang="en">
  <head>
    <meta charset="UTF-8" />
    <title>Example 10 - (Convert square texture to isometric diamond)</title>

    <script>
      window.onload = function () {
        var canvas = document.getElementById('myCanvas');
        var c = canvas.getContext('2d');

        var texture = new Image();
        texture.src = '../img/squareTexture.png';

        drawDiamond();

        function drawDiamond() {
          // Save the current context
          c.save();

          // Scale the results to a isometric/dimetric 2:1 ratio
          c.scale(1, 0.5);

          // Rotate the context 45 degrees
          c.rotate(45 * Math.PI / 180);

          // If we rotate the image on 0, 0 half of it will be
          // displayed outside the canvas, so compensate
          c.drawImage(texture,
                      0,
                      0,
                      texture.width,
                      texture.height,
                      texture.width / 2,
                      (texture.height / 2) * -1,
                      texture.width,
                      texture.height);

          // Restore the context
          c.restore();
        }
      }
    </script>
  </head>
  <body>
    <canvas id="myCanvas" width="300" height="300"></canvas>
  </body>
</html>
```

Figure 2-3. The output of Example 2-1

If we combine the `drawDiamond()` function with the HTML5 Canvas `getImageData()` and `putImageData()` functions that we discussed in the previous chapter, we can store the result of the transformation and later reuse it to display many elements using only a single transformation.

The problem is that using `putImageData()` is slower than calling `drawImage()`, so a more efficient approach (even if it is an small inconvenience for our texture artists) is to use diamond-shaped images directly.

Drawing and working inside of an isometric grid is not hard if you know how isometric tiles work, as shown in Figure 2-4.

As you can see, an isometric tile is nothing more than a rectangle that is twice as wide as it is tall. The diamond inside of it, usually just an image or a vector representation, is defined by the coordinates:

West
    X: 0
    Y: `tile.height`/2
East
    X: `tile.width`
    Y: `tile.height`/2

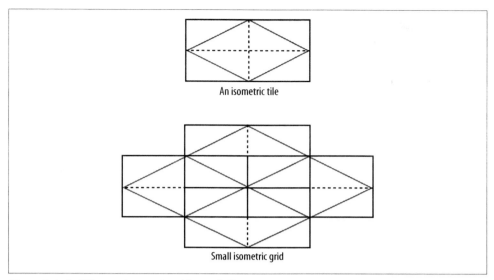

An isometric tile

Small isometric grid

Figure 2-4. Building an isometric grid out of tiles

North

X: `tile.width/2`

Y: 0

South

X: `tile.width/2`

Y: `tile.height`

This means that if we want to display two tiles:

1. We first need to position the first tile.
2. The second tile should be positioned in the first tile's width divided by 2, plus the first tile's height divided by 2.

Also, due to how this process works, we need to keep in mind that tiles must have an even width (divisible by 2); otherwise, we won't be able to form the grid in a consistent way.

Example 2-2 shows how to display a basic isometric grid. Later on, we'll modify it so that it uses the high-performance approach.

Example 2-2. A simple but inefficient approach to displaying an isometric grid

```
<!DOCTYPE html>
<html lang="en">
  <head>
    <meta charset="UTF-8" />
    <title>Example 11 - (Displaying an isometric grid)</title>
```

```
<script>
  window.onload = function () {
    var canvas = document.getElementById('myCanvas');
    var c = canvas.getContext('2d');

    var tile = new Image();
    tile.src = "../img/tile.png";

    draw();

    function draw() {

      c.clearRect (0, 0, canvas.width, canvas.height);

      for (var col = 0; col < 10; col++) {
        for (var row = 0; row < 10; row++) {
          var tilePositionX = (row - col) * tile.height;

          // Center the grid horizontally
          tilePositionX += (canvas.width / 2) - (tile.width / 2);

          var tilePositionY = (row + col) * (tile.height / 2);

          c.drawImage(tile,
                      Math.round(tilePositionX),
                      Math.round(tilePositionY),
                      tile.width,
                      tile.height);
        }
      }
    }
  }
</script>
</head>
<body>
  <canvas id="myCanvas" width="600" height="300"></canvas>
</body>
</html>
```

Translating click coordinates to matrix coordinates in an isometric grid is a bit more complex than doing it in a square grid, especially if we're dealing with an infinite grid. For the sake of simplicity and performance, these examples (and our final game) will use a fixed grid of 250×250 (62,500 tiles), which is bigger than other games of this genre.

Before we make the formula, we need to take into account the offset produced by centering the grid horizontally (Figure 2-6).

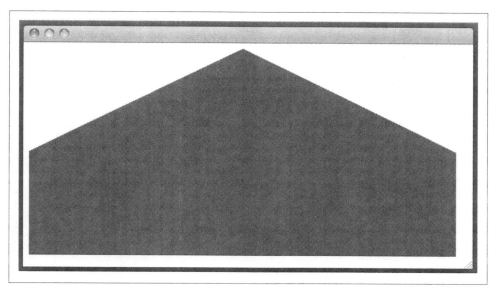

Figure 2-5. Output of Example 2-2

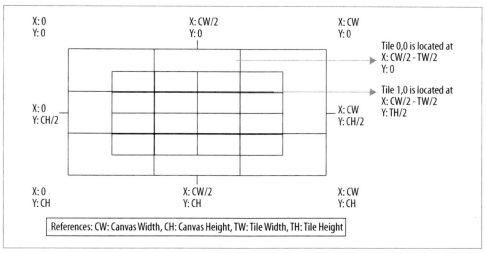

Figure 2-6. We can see how the tiles are going to be positioned on the canvas and how we can calculate on which tile we clicked on

We first need to take into account any offsets in the X or Y axes such as scroll positions or horizontal/vertical alignments. Any offsets not taken into account will cause problems when we translate the coordinates:

```
var gridOffsetY = grid.height;
var gridOffsetX = grid.width;

// Take into account the offset on the X axis caused
// by centering the grid horizontally
gridOffsetX += (canvas.width / 2) - (tile.width / 2);
```

Using these two variables, we can start translating the coordinates for the column:

```
var col = (e.clientY - gridOffsetY) * 2;
col = ((gridOffsetX + col) - e.clientX) / 2;
```

And having the column, we can do the same for the rows:

```
var row = ((e.clientX + col) - tile.height) - gridOffsetX;
```

We finally finish by dividing both results by the tile height and rounding the result:

```
row = Math.round(row / tile.height);
col = Math.round(col / tile.height);
```

Example 2-3 applies this formula in a practical context, placing tiles to create the image shown in Figure 2-7.

Example 2-3. Converting click coordinates to matrix coordinates

```
<!DOCTYPE html>
<html lang="en">
  <head>
    <meta charset="UTF-8" />
    <title>Example 12 - (Capturing click events and translating them
        to matrix coordinates)</title>

    <script>
      window.onload = function () {
        var grid = {
          width: 10,
          height: 10
        }

        var canvas = document.getElementById('myCanvas');
        var c = canvas.getContext('2d');

        var tileMap = [];

        var tile = new Image();
        tile.src = "../img/tile.png";

        var dirt = new Image();
        dirt.src = "../img/dirt.png";

        canvas.addEventListener('mousedown', handleMouseDown, false);
```

```
        draw();

    function handleMouseDown(e) {
      var gridOffsetY = grid.height;
      var gridOffsetX = grid.width;

      // Take into account the offset on the X axis caused
      // by centering the grid horizontally
      gridOffsetX += (canvas.width / 2) - (tile.width / 2);

      var col = (e.clientY - gridOffsetY) * 2;
      col = ((gridOffsetX + col) - e.clientX) / 2;

      var row = ((e.clientX + col) - tile.height) - gridOffsetX;

      row = Math.round(row / tile.height);
      col = Math.round(col / tile.height);

      // Check the boundaries!
      if (row >= 0 &&
        col >= 0 &&
        row <= grid.width &&
        col <= grid.height) {

        tileMap[row] = (tileMap[row] === undefined) ? [] : tileMap[row];

        tileMap[row][col] = 1;
        draw();
      }
    }


    function draw() {

      c.clearRect (0, 0, canvas.width, canvas.height);

      for (var col = 0; col < grid.height; col++) {
        for (var row = 0; row < grid.width; row++) {

          var tilePositionX = (row - col) * tile.height;

          // Center the grid horizontally
          tilePositionX += (canvas.width / 2) - (tile.width / 2);

          var tilePositionY = (row + col) * (tile.height / 2);

          if (tileMap[row] != null && tileMap[row][col] != null) {
            c.drawImage(dirt,
                        Math.round(tilePositionX),
                        Math.round(tilePositionY),
                        dirt.width,
                        dirt.height);
          } else {
            c.drawImage(tile, Math.round(tilePositionX), Math.round(tilePositionY),
tile.width, tile.height);
```

```
                }
              }
            }
          }
        }
      </script>
    </head>
    <body>
      <canvas id="myCanvas" width="600" height="300"></canvas>
    </body>
</html>
```

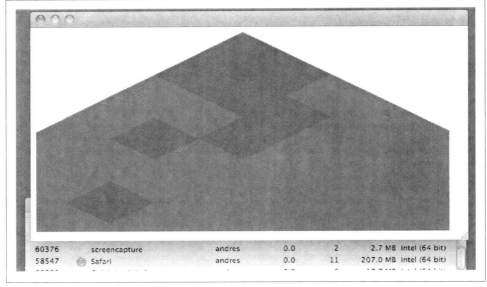

Figure 2-7. Using the new tile display approach; CPU usage is at 0%

In the code repository is an example called *ex12-isogrid-click-alt.html*, which shows how to perform a matrix rotation.

Now that you know how to translate click coordinates to matrix coordinates in an isometric plane, one thing that we might want to do is to place buildings, like the one shown in Figure 2-8.

Figure 2-8. A building texture occupying four tiles

Unlike conventional tiles, building textures like the one seen in Figures 2-8 and 2-9 have different heights and may occupy more than one tile, which requires a different approach to position them.

As you can see in Figure 2-9, in order to be displayed correctly, buildings should be positioned starting on the bottom-center coordinate, as follows:

```
for (var row = 0; row < 10; row++) {
  for (var col = 0; col < 10; col++) {

    var tilePositionX = (row - col) * tile.height;

    // Center the grid horizontally
    tilePositionX += (canvas.width / 2) - (tile.width / 2);

    var tilePositionY = (row + col) * (tile.height / 2);

    if (tileMap[row] != null && tileMap[row][col] != null) {
      tilePositionY -= building.height - tile.height;
      tilePositionX -= (building.width / 2) - (tile.width / 2);
      c.drawImage(building,
                  Math.round(tilePositionX),
                  Math.round(tilePositionY),
                  building.width,
                  building.height);
    } else {
      c.drawImage(tile, Math.round(tilePositionX), Math.round(tilePositionY),
tile.width, tile.height);
    }
  }
}
```

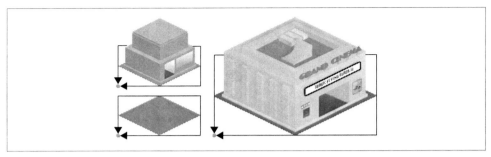

Figure 2-9. Placing buildings on the bottom center of the tile

The entire example is available in the code repository, called *ex13-isogrid-buildings.html*.

So far, we have used the grid only to store whether something should be shown or not: we're only keeping track of which tiles are occupied, not what's placed on them. Obviously, our game will need a more complex object structure, especially if we want to place buildings that occupy more than one tile, such as a cinema (2×2 tiles) or a hotel (2×2).

The approach that we're going to use in order to prevent the user from placing buildings on top of each other will be to check whether the tile on which the user clicked contains an special object (called `BuildingPortion`) that will give us a set of coordinates to the main tile that contains the "real" building object. Figure 2-10 shows this concept.

	1	2	3	4
1		objId: 2 x: -1 y: 0		Building objId: 1 **type: C**
2			objId: 4 x: 0 y: -1	objId: 4 x: -1 y: -1
3	objId: 3 x: 0 y: -1	objId: 3 x: -1 y: -1	Building objId: 4 **type: A**	objId: 4 x: -1 y: 0
4	Building objId: 3 **type: A**	objId: 3 x: -1 y: 0		

Figure 2-10. Calculating building locations

In Figure 2-10:

- Buildings of type A (such as objId = 3 or 4) have a dimension of 2×2 tiles.
- Buildings of type B have a dimension of 2×1 tiles (objId = 2).
- Buildings of type C have a dimension of 1×1 tiles (objId = 1).

Querying the position 3, 2 in the grid, for example, would indicate that if we move one tile to the left and one tile down, we're going to find the building with objId = 3. These positions are created automatically when we place each building.

Example 2-4 (*ex13-isogrid-buildings-alt.html*) shows how to implement this idea, and you can see the result in Figure 2-11.

Example 2-4. Implementing building location tracking

```
<!DOCTYPE html>
<html lang="en">
  <head>
    <meta charset="UTF-8" />
    <title>Example 13 - (Placing buildings)</title>

    <script>
      var Cinema = function(instanceId) {
        this.buildingTypeId = 1; // It's a cinema
        this.instanceId = null;

        this.texture = new Image();
        this.texture.src = "../img/cinema.png";

        this.width = this.texture.width;
        this.height = this.texture.height;

        this.tileWidth = 2;
        this.tileHeight = 2;
      }

      var BuildingPortion = function(buildingTypeId, x, y) {
        this.buildingTypeId = buildingTypeId;
        this.x = x;
        this.y = y;
      }

      window.onload = function () {
        var grid = {
          width: 10,
          height: 10
        }

        var canvas = document.getElementById('myCanvas');
        var c = canvas.getContext('2d');

        var tileMap = [];
```

```
var tile = new Image();
tile.src = "../img/tile.png";

var buildingCounter = 0; // In reality, the building count is being
                         // performed on the server side
                         // in the database

canvas.addEventListener('mousedown', handleMouseDown, false);

draw();

function handleMouseDown(e) {
  var gridOffsetY = grid.height;
  var gridOffsetX = grid.width;

  // Take into account the offset on the X axis
  // caused by centering the grid horizontally
  gridOffsetX += (canvas.width / 2) - (tile.width / 2);

  var col = (e.clientY - gridOffsetY) * 2;
  col = ((gridOffsetX + col) - e.clientX) / 2;

  var row = ((e.clientX + col) - tile.height) - gridOffsetX;

  row = Math.round(row / tile.height);
  col = Math.round(col / tile.height);

  // Create the building object
  var cinema = new Cinema(buildingCounter);

  // Check the boundaries!
  if (row >= 0 &&
    col >= 0 &&
    row <= grid.width &&
    col <= grid.height) {

    tileMap[row] = (tileMap[row] === undefined) ? [] : tileMap[row];

    // Do we have enough space to place this building on the grid?
    if (((row+1) - cinema.tileWidth) < 0 || ((col+1) - cinema.tileHeight) < 0) {
    alert("Invalid Location!\nPart of the building will appear outside the grid.");
      return;
    }

    // Now check that the tiles that the building
    // will occupy are not occupied by other buildings
    for (var i = (row+1) - cinema.tileWidth; i <= row; i++) {
      for (var j = (col+1) - cinema.tileHeight; j <= col; j++) {
        if (tileMap[i] != undefined && tileMap[i][j] != null) {
          alert("There's another building there!")
          return;
        }
      }
    }
```

```
        // Place the building
        for (var i = (row+1) - cinema.tileWidth; i <= row; i++) {
          for (var j = (col+1) - cinema.tileHeight; j <= col; j++) {
            tileMap[i] = (tileMap[i] == undefined) ? [] : tileMap[i];

            tileMap[i][j] = (i == row && j == col) ? // Forced line break
                        cinema :                    // Forced line break
                        new BuildingPortion(cinema.buildingTypeId, i, j);
          }
        }

        buildingCounter++;

        draw();
      }
    }


    function draw() {

      c.clearRect (0, 0, canvas.width, canvas.height);

      for (var col = 0; col < 10; col++) {
        for (var row = 0; row < 10; row++) {

          var tilePositionX = (row - col) * tile.height;

          // Center the grid horizontally
          tilePositionX += (canvas.width / 2) - (tile.width / 2);

          var tilePositionY = (row + col) * (tile.height / 2);

          if (tileMap[row] != null && tileMap[row][col] != null) {
            tilePositionY -= tileMap[row][col].height - tile.height;
            tilePositionX -= (tileMap[row][col].width / 2) - (tile.width / 2);

            if (!(tileMap[row][col] instanceof BuildingPortion)) {
                c.drawImage(tileMap[row][col].texture,
                        Math.round(tilePositionX),
                        Math.round(tilePositionY),
                        tileMap[row][col].width,
                        tileMap[row][col].height);
            }
          } else {
              c.drawImage(tile, Math.round(tilePositionX), Math.round(tilePositionY),
tile.width, tile.height);
          }
        }
      }
    }
  }
  </script>
 </head>
 <body>
  <canvas id="myCanvas" width="600" height="300"></canvas>
```

```
    </body>
</html>
```

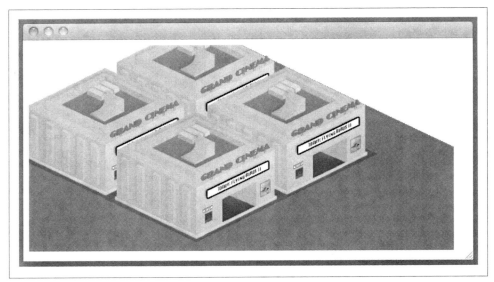

Figure 2-11. Screenshot of Example 2-4

Unlike the rectangular grid used in previous sections, showing only the tiles that we need on an isometric grid requires a bit more work and additional iterations. Figure 2-12 shows that if we scroll up and start the column iterations on 1 instead of 0, there's an entire set of tiles that will not show up, as they depend on both column and row iterations.

An easy way to solve this situation is to use our click routine again and grab the tiles that are being shown in the top-left, top-right, bottom-left, and bottom-right corners in the following way:

```
var pos_TL = translatePixelsToMatrix(canvas, tile, 1, 1);
var pos_BL = translatePixelsToMatrix(canvas, tile, 1, canvas.height);
var pos_TR = translatePixelsToMatrix(canvas, tile, canvas.width, 1);
var pos_BR = translatePixelsToMatrix(canvas, tile, canvas.width, canvas.height);

var startRow = pos_TL.row;
var startCol = pos_TR.col;
var rowCount = pos_BR.row + 1;
var colCount = pos_BL.col + 1;

startRow = (startRow < 0) ? 0 : startRow;
startCol = (startCol < 0) ? 0 : startCol;

// Place the artificial limit
rowCount = (rowCount > grid.width) ? grid.width : rowCount;
colCount = (colCount > grid.height) ? grid.height : colCount;
```

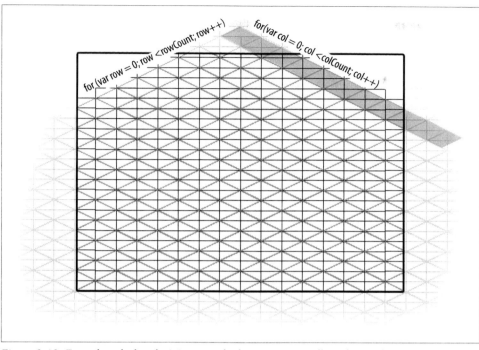

Figure 2-12. Even though the tile 0,0 is outside the screen, we still need to cycle through column 0 (and row 0); otherwise, some of the other tiles (that should be printed) won't be shown

```
for (var row = startRow; row < rowCount; row++) {
    for (var col = startCol; col < colCount; col++) {

        // ...
    }
}
```

The translatePixelsToMatrix() function looks like this:

```
function translatePixelsToMatrix(canvas, tile, x, y) {
  var gridOffsetY = (grid.height * zoomHelper.level) + scrollPosition.y;
  var gridOffsetX = (grid.width * zoomHelper.level);

  // By default the grid appears centered horizontally
  gridOffsetX += (canvas.width / 2) - ((tile.width / 2) * zoomHelper.level) +
scrollPosition.x;

  var col = (2 * (y - gridOffsetY) - x + gridOffsetX) / 2;
  var row = x + col - gridOffsetX - tile.height;

  col = Math.round(col / tile.height);
  row = Math.round(row / tile.height);
```

```
    return {
      row: row,
      col: col
    }
  }
```

We will use this improved approach in the next chapters as well as in the final game.

CHAPTER 3

Interface Considerations

There's much more to building a great-looking game than just laying out buildings on a grid. A working game requires ways for users to communicate with the game, and as games move toward mobile delivery, that need for communication changes. User expectations of mobile devices are often different from their expectations of desktop computers, and the devices themselves add new complexities.

GUI Design and Interaction in Web Games

Graphical user interface (GUI) and human-computer interaction (HCI) are extremely critical areas in application development but are sometimes overlooked by developers. Companies and applications such as Apple, Google, and Facebook were able to become successful in part due to their excellent design usability guidelines. They require consistency, simplicity, responsiveness, and minimal design across all their products. Of course, video games (including ours) are no exception to this rule, but there is one big gotcha that you need to keep in mind: unlike other sorts of applications, our GUI has to be comfortably usable on both desktop and mobile devices.

Knowing this, we can work out a simple set of recommendations to follow when designing it:

- We can't rely on mouse hovers to give feedback or to present tooltips. Touchscreens have only two states: either you are touching the screen or you aren't.

- Having no tooltips means that icons and buttons must communicate very clearly what they are going to do.

- We can't rely on right clicks either, as mobile devices won't have that functionality.

- In isometric games, presenting the game in landscape mode is a better use of screen real state than presenting it in portrait mode.

- Important information, such as the account balance, is better displayed on the top and navigational elements are better displayed on the bottom-left corner. (Remember that 90% of the world is right-handed, and they'll probably be using their left hand to hold the device while they use their able hand, the right one, to click, as shown in Figure 3-1.)

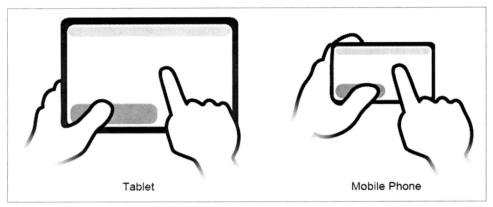

Figure 3-1. Phone as held by the right-handed majority

- Due to the very small size of mobile phones, we should keep interface clutter to an absolute minimum.
- We're going to assume that scrolling down/up with your PC's mouse is the same as zooming in/out with two fingers (almost a standard practice nowadays).
- We're also going to avoid presenting floating windows and will use scrollable panels instead. These panels will appear on the right of the screen.

 Some HCI and user experience (UE) guidelines for mobile devices include the following:

- iOS Human Interface Guidelines, by Apple: *http://developer.apple.com/library/ios/#documentation/UserExperience/Conceptual/MobileHIG/Introduction/Introduction.html*
- User Experience Guidelines, by Google (for Android devices): *http://developer.android.com/guide/practices/ui_guidelines/index.html*

In essence, our application GUI will look similar to Figure 3-2.

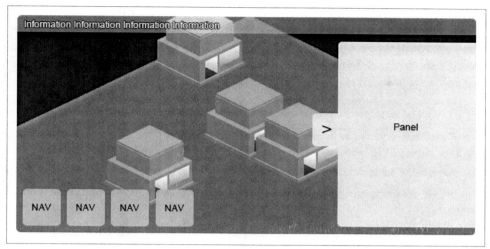

Figure 3-2. A rough sketch of the interface

Each of the navigation buttons will enable a tool or perform a particular action. In our game, we're going to be adding the following tools:

- A Select tool to select individual buildings
- A Move button that toggles the scroll position modifier, which can be used with the mouse or by dragging a finger across the screen when using a mobile device or a tablet
- Zoom In and Zoom Out buttons that will allows us to enlarge the grid and the object inside it, when we click on the screen
- A Rotate button to rotate the values of the matrix counterclockwise
- A Demolish button to destroy a specific building

Additionally, we're going to add support for the following features:

- Using the mouse wheel to zoom in or zoom out without having to toggle the zoom buttons
- Using the keys on our keyboard to scroll the grid or to zoom in, zoom out, or rotate the grid

Implementing the GUI

The HEAD section of the HTML code of our page is also going to include some special tags.

Because we're going to be handling the zooming in a different way than the one included by default in some mobile browsers, we need to disable the default functionality completely:

```
<meta name="viewport" content="width=device-width, initial-scale=1, user-
scalable=no" />
```

Devices like the Apple iPhone, Apple iPad, and some Android phones allow the user
to add our site to their home screen. We can change the icon of our application by using
the following tags:

```
<link rel="apple-touch-icon" href="../img/touristResortIcon.png" />
<link rel="apple-touch-icon-precomposed" href="../img/touristResortIcon.png"/>
```

If the user has added the application to her home screen, there's a way to hide the
browser chrome GUI such as a the URL bar, back/forward buttons, and so on:

```
<meta name="apple-mobile-web-app-capable" content="yes" />
```

Finally, we are going to add the Google Chrome frame tag to display our game in older
browsers:

```
<meta http-equiv="X-UA-Compatible" content="chrome=1" />
```

The GUI will be contained inside a div with its id attribute set to ui. Then we can listen
for any events happening to it or any of its child elements:

```
var ui = document.getElementById('ui');

// Listen GUI events
ui.addEventListener('mouseup', handler, false);
```

The HTML code of our GUI is going to look like this:

```
<div id="ui">
  <div id="top">
      Account Balance: <span id="balance">0</span> Coins
  </div>
  <div id="tools">
    <ul>
      <li id="select"></li>
      <li id="move"></li>
      <li id="zoomIn"></li>
      <li id="zoomOut"></li>
      <li id="rotate"></li>
      <li id="demolish"></li>
    </ul>
  </div>
  <div id="panel-container" class="hidden">
    <a href="javascript:void(0)" id="panel-toggle">Build</a>
    <div id="panel">
      <h3>Choose a building:</h3>
      <ul id="buildings">
        <li>
          <h2>Building Name</h2>
          <p>
            Description
            <br />
            <span>$Cost</span>
          </p>
        </li>
```

```
      <li>
        <h2>Building Name</h2>
        <p>
          Description
          <br />
          <span>$Cost</span>
        </p>
      </li>

      <li>
        <h2>Building Name</h2>
        <p>
          Description
          <br />
          <span>$Cost</span>
        </p>
      </li>
    </ul>
  </div>
  </div>
</div>
```

And the click handling function is going to look like this:

```
var ui = document.getElementById('ui');

// Listen for GUI events
ui.addEventListener('mouseup', function(e) {
  switch(e.target.getAttribute('id')) {
    case 'panel-toggle':
      // ...
      break;
    case 'select':
      // ...
      break;
    case 'move':
      // ...
      break;
    case 'zoomIn':
      // ...
      break;
    case 'zoomOut':
      // ...
      break;
    case 'rotate':
      // ...
      break;
    case 'demolish':
      // ...
      break;
  }
}, false);
```

Notice that the HTML code shown before the panel and the account balance contains faux values; don't worry, we'll populate these with real values later on when we integrate the client-side scripts with the server-side scripts.

Mobile devices will detect click, mouseDown, mouseMove, mouseUp, and DOMMouseScroll events, but impose a penalty of between 250 and 600 milliseconds depending on the hardware. In order to alleviate this issue, we need to detect whether the device supports touch events, then use native touch and gesture events such as touchstart, touchmove, and touchend, and detect gestures by using gesturestart or gestureend.

We can detect and manage both clicks and touch events by using the Modernizr library. Modernizr.touch returns true if the device supports touch events, which means that we can do this:

```
var pointer = {
  DOWN: 'mousedown',
  UP: 'mouseup',
  MOVE: 'mousemove'
};

if (Modernizr.touch){
  pointer.DOWN = 'touchstart';
  pointer.UP = 'touchend';
  pointer.MOVE = 'touchmove';
}

window.addEventListener('resize', function() { doResize(canvas); }, false);
canvas.addEventListener(pointer.DOWN, handleMouseDown, false);
canvas.addEventListener(pointer.MOVE, handleDrag, false);
document.body.addEventListener(pointer.UP, handleMouseUp, false);

if (Modernizr.touch){
  // Detect gestures
  document.body.addEventListener('gestureend', handleGestureEnd, false);

} else {
  document.body.addEventListener('keydown', handleKeyDown, false);

  // Detect scrolling
  document.body.addEventListener('mousewheel', handleScroll, false);
  document.body.addEventListener('DOMMouseScroll', handleScroll, false);

}
```

Now that our codebase is getting bigger and more complex, we're also going to create a Game class to simplify the amount of work; we'll also divide the code on the page into multiple scripts.

The complete code in Example 3-1 is online as *ex14-gui.html* in the official code repository. See Figure 3-3. You can also find *ex14-gui-sound.html* in the code repository; it is the same example with music playing in the background.

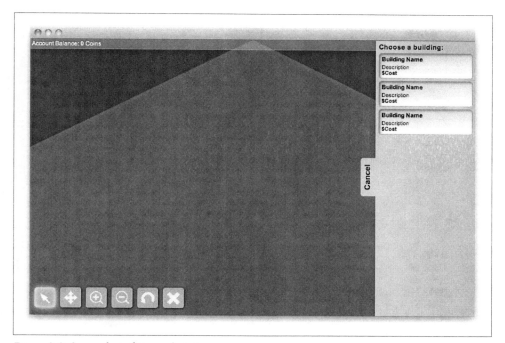

Figure 3-3. Screenshot of Example 3-1

Example 3-1. GUI (HTML)

```
<!DOCTYPE html>
<html lang="en">
  <head>
    <meta charset="UTF-8" />

    <!-- We'll take care of the zoom ourselves -->
    <meta name="viewport" content="width=device-width,initial-scale=1,
user-scalable=no" />

    <!-- iPhone icon + chromeless browser -->
    <meta name="apple-mobile-web-app-capable" content="yes" />

    <!-- iPhone homescreen icon -->
    <link rel="apple-touch-icon" href="../img/touristResortIcon.png" />
    <link rel="apple-touch-icon-precomposed" href="../img/touristResortIcon.png"/>

    <!-- Chrome Frame -->
    <meta http-equiv="X-UA-Compatible" content="chrome=1" />

    <title>Example 14 - Graphical User Interface</title>

    <link rel="stylesheet" href="ui-style.css" />
    <script src="../utils/modernizr-1.7.min.js" charset="utf-8"></script>
    <script src="game-ex14.js" charset="utf-8"></script>
    <script>
```

```
// Enums
var Keys = {
  UP: 38,
  DOWN: 40,
  LEFT: 37,
  RIGHT: 39,
  W: 87,
  A: 65,
  S: 83,
  D: 68,
  Z: 90,
  X: 88,
  R: 82
}

var Tools = {
  current: 4, // Default tool
  /* - */
  MOVE: 0,
  ZOOM_IN: 1,
  ZOOM_OUT: 2,
  DEMOLISH: 3,
  SELECT: 4,
  BUILD: 5
}

window.onload = function () {

  var canvas = document.getElementById('gameCanvas');
  var game = document.getElementById('game');

  // Initialize the game object
  var g = new Game(canvas, game, 500, 500);

  var pointer = {
    DOWN: 'mousedown',
    UP: 'mouseup',
    MOVE: 'mousemove'
  };

  if (Modernizr.touch){
    pointer.DOWN = 'touchstart';
    pointer.UP = 'touchend';
    pointer.MOVE = 'touchmove';
  }

  // Set up the event listeners
  window.addEventListener('resize', function() {
        g.doResize();
    }, false);
  canvas.addEventListener(pointer.DOWN, function(e) {
        g.handleMouseDown(e);
    }, false);
```

```
        canvas.addEventListener(pointer.MOVE, function(e) {
            g.handleDrag(e);
        }, false);
        document.body.addEventListener(pointer.UP, function(e) {
            g.handleMouseUp(e);
        }, false);

    if (Modernizr.touch){
        // Detect gestures
        document.body.addEventListener('gestureend', function(e)
{ g.handleGestureEnd(e); }, false);

    } else {
        document.body.addEventListener('keydown', function(e) { g.handleKeyDown(e); },
false);

        // Detect mousewheel scrolling
        document.body.addEventListener('mousewheel', function(e) { g.handleScroll(e); },
false);
        document.body.addEventListener('DOMMouseScroll', function(e)
{ g.handleScroll(e); }, false);

    }

    // Listen for GUI events
    var ui = document.getElementById('ui');
    ui.addEventListener(pointer.UP, function(e) {
        switch(e.target.getAttribute('id')) {
            case 'panel-toggle':
                var panelContainer = document.getElementById('panel-container');
                var classes = panelContainer.getAttribute('class');

                if (classes != null && classes.length > 0) {
                    panelContainer.setAttribute('class', '');
                    document.getElementById('panel-toggle').innerHTML = 'Cancel';
                } else {
                    panelContainer.setAttribute('class', 'hidden');
                    document.getElementById('panel-toggle').innerHTML = 'Build';
                }
                break;
            case 'select':
                selectTool(Tools.SELECT, document.getElementById('select'));
                break;
            case 'move':
                selectTool(Tools.MOVE, document.getElementById('move'));
                break;
            case 'zoomIn':
                selectTool(Tools.ZOOM_IN, document.getElementById('zoomIn'));
                break;
            case 'zoomOut':
                selectTool(Tools.ZOOM_OUT, document.getElementById('zoomOut'));
                break;
            case 'rotate':
                g.rotateGrid();
                g.draw();
```

```
          break;
        case 'demolish':
          selectTool(Tools.DEMOLISH, document.getElementById('demolish'));
          break;
        default:
          // He didn't click on any option and actually click
          // on an empty section of the UI, fallback to the canvas.
          e.srcElement = canvas;
          e.target = canvas;
          e.toElement = canvas;

          g.handleMouseDown(e);

          break;
      }
    }, false);
  }

  function selectTool(tool, elem) {

    // Remove the "active" class from any element inside the div#tools ul
    for (var i = 0, x = elem.parentNode.childNodes.length; i < x; i++) {
      if (elem.parentNode.childNodes[i].tagName == "LI") {
        elem.parentNode.childNodes[i].className = null;
      }
    }

    elem.className += "active";

    switch(tool) {
      case Tools.SELECT:
        Tools.current = Tools.SELECT;
        break;
      case Tools.MOVE:
        Tools.current = Tools.MOVE;
        break;
      case Tools.ZOOM_IN:
        Tools.current = Tools.ZOOM_IN;
        break;
      case Tools.ZOOM_OUT:
        Tools.current = Tools.ZOOM_OUT;
        break;
      case Tools.DEMOLISH:
        Tools.current = Tools.DEMOLISH;
        break;
    }

  }
</script>
</head>
<body>
  <div id="game">

  <canvas id="gameCanvas" width="1" height="1"></canvas>
  <div id="ui">
```

```html
    <div id="top">
      Account Balance: <span id="balance">0</span> Coins
    </div>
    <div id="tools">
      <ul>
        <li id="select" class="active"></li>
        <li id="move"></li>
        <li id="zoomIn"></li>
        <li id="zoomOut"></li>
        <li id="rotate"></li>
        <li id="demolish"></li>
      </ul>
    </div>
    <div id="panel-container" class="hidden">
      <a href="javascript:void(0)" id="panel-toggle">Build</a>
      <div id="panel">
        <h3>Choose a building:</h3>
        <ul id="buildings">
          <li>
            <h2>Building Name</h2>
            <p>
              Description
              <br />
              <span>$Cost</span>
            </p>
          </li>

          <li>
            <h2>Building Name</h2>
            <p>
              Description
              <br />
              <span>$Cost</span>
            </p>
          </li>

          <li>
            <h2>Building Name</h2>
            <p>
              Description
              <br />
              <span>$Cost</span>
            </p>
          </li>
        </ul>
      </div>
    </div>
  </div>

  </div>
  </body>
</html>
```

Example 3-2. Game function (JavaScript)

```javascript
// Game class for example 14
function Game(canvas, game, gridSizeW, gridSizeH) {
    this.started = true;
    this.gameContainer = game;
    this.canvas = canvas;

    // Get the 2D Context
    this.c = canvas.getContext('2d');

    // Can we run the game?
    var missingDeps = [];
    var dependencies = [Modernizr.rgba,
                        Modernizr.canvas,
                        Modernizr.borderradius,
                        Modernizr.boxshadow,
                        Modernizr.cssgradients];

    for (var i = 0, dep = dependencies.length; i < dep; i++) {
        if (!dependencies[i]) {
            missingDeps.push(dependencies[i]);
        }
    }

    if (missingDeps.length !== 0) {
        var msg = "This browser doesn't include some of the ";
        msg += "technologies needed to play the game";
        alert(msg);
        this.started = false;
        return;
    }

    // Tile texture
    this.tile = new Image();
    this.tile.src = "../img/tile.png";

    // Grid dimensions
    this.grid = {
        width: gridSizeW,
        height: gridSizeH
    }

    // Tile map matrix
    this.tileMap = [];

    // Drag helper
    this.dragHelper = {
        active: false,
        x: 0,
        y: 0
    }

    // Zoom helper, 3 zoom levels supported
    this.zoomHelper = {
        level: 1,
```

```
            NORMAL: 1,
            FAR: 0.50,
            CLOSE: 2
        }

        // Scroll position helper, keeps track of scrolling
        this.scrollPosition = { x: 0, y: 0 }

        // Default zoom level
        this.tile.width *= this.zoomHelper.level;
        this.tile.height *= this.zoomHelper.level;

        // Initially center the starting point horizontally and vertically
        var nspy = (this.grid.height * this.zoomHelper.level) + this.scrollPosition.y;
        var nspx = (this.grid.width * this.zoomHelper.level) + this.scrollPosition.x;
        this.scrollPosition.y -= nspy;
        this.scrollPosition.x -= nspx;

        this.doResize();
        this.draw();
}

Game.prototype.handleGestureEnd = function(e) {
    e.preventDefault();

    if (Math.floor(e.scale) == 0) {
        this.zoomIn();
    } else {
        this.zoomOut();
    }
}

Game.prototype.handleScroll = function(e) {
    e.preventDefault();

    var scrollValue = (e.wheelDelta == undefined) ? e.detail * -1 : e.wheelDelta;

    if (scrollValue >= 0) {
        this.zoomInt();
    } else {
        this.zoomOut();
    }
}

Game.prototype.handleKeyDown = function(e) {
    switch (e.keyCode) {
        case Keys.UP:
        case Keys.W:
            this.scrollPosition.y += 20;
            break;
        case Keys.DOWN:
        case Keys.S:
            this.scrollPosition.y -= 20;
            break;
```

```
                case Keys.LEFT:
                case Keys.A:
                    this.scrollPosition.x += 20;
                    break;
                case Keys.RIGHT:
                case Keys.D:
                    this.scrollPosition.x -= 20;
                    break;
                case Keys.X:
                    this.zoomIn();
                    break;
                case Keys.Z:
                    this.zoomOut();
                    break;
                case Keys.R:
                    this.rotateGrid();
                    break;
        }

        this.draw();
}

Game.prototype.handleDrag = function(e) {
        var x, y;
        e.preventDefault();

        if (Modernizr.touch) {
                x = e.touches[0].pageX;
                y = e.touches[0].pageY;
        } else {
                x = e.clientX;
                y = e.clientY;
        }

        switch (Tools.current) {
                case Tools.MOVE:
                        if (this.dragHelper.active) {
                                // Smooth scrolling effect
                                this.scrollPosition.x -= (this.dragHelper.x - x) / 18;
                                this.scrollPosition.y -= (this.dragHelper.y - x) / 18;
                        }
                        this.draw();
                        break;
        }
}

Game.prototype.handleMouseUp = function(e) {
    e.preventDefault();

    switch (Tools.current) {
        case Tools.MOVE:
            this.dragHelper.active = false;
            break;
    }
}
```

```
Game.prototype.handleMouseDown = function(e) {
    var x, y;
    e.preventDefault();

    if (Modernizr.touch) {
        x = e.touches[0].pageX;
        y = e.touches[0].pageY;
    } else {
        x = e.clientX;
        y = e.clientY;
    }

    switch (Tools.current) {
        case Tools.BUILD:

            break;
        case Tools.MOVE:
            this.dragHelper.active = true;
            this.dragHelper.x = x;
            this.dragHelper.y = y;
            break;
        case Tools.ZOOM_IN:
            this.zoomIn();
            break;
        case Tools.ZOOM_OUT:
            this.zoomOut();
            break;
        case Tools.DEMOLISH:

            var pos = this.translatePixelsToMatrix(x, y);

            if (this.tileMap[pos.row] != undefined &&
              this.tileMap[pos.row][pos.col] != undefined) {
                this.tileMap[pos.row][pos.col] = null;
            }

            break;
    }

    this.draw();
}

Game.prototype.doResize = function() {

    this.canvas.width = document.body.clientWidth;
    this.canvas.height = document.body.clientHeight;


    this.draw();
}

Game.prototype.translatePixelsToMatrix = function(x, y) {
    var tileHeight = this.tile.height * this.zoomHelper.level;
    var tileWidth = this.tile.width * this.zoomHelper.level;
```

```
        var zoomedHeight = (this.grid.height * this.zoomHelper.level);
        var gridOffsetY = zoomedHeight + this.scrollPosition.y;
        var gridOffsetX = (this.grid.width * this.zoomHelper.level);

        // By default the grid appears centered horizontally
        var zoomedWidth = ((tileWidth / 2) * this.zoomHelper.level;
        gridOffsetX += (this.canvas.width / 2) - zoomedWidth) + this.scrollPosition.x;

        var col = (2 * (y - gridOffsetY) - x + gridOffsetX) / 2;
        var row = x + col - gridOffsetX - tileHeight;

        col = Math.round(col / tileHeight);
        row = Math.round(row / tileHeight);

        return {
            row: row,
            col: col
        }
}

Game.prototype.draw = function(srcX, srcY, destX, destY) {
    srcX = (srcX === undefined) ? 0 : srcX;
    srcY = (srcY === undefined) ? 0 : srcY;
    destX = (destX === undefined) ? this.canvas.width : destX;
    destY = (destY === undefined) ? this.canvas.height : destY;

    this.c.clearRect (0, 0, this.canvas.width, this.canvas.height);
    this.c.fillStyle = '#0C3B00'; // Green background
    this.c.fillRect (0, 0, this.canvas.width, this.canvas.height);

    var pos_TL = this.translatePixelsToMatrix(1, 1);
    var pos_BL = this.translatePixelsToMatrix(1, this.canvas.height);
    var pos_TR = this.translatePixelsToMatrix(this.canvas.width, 1);
    var pos_BR = this.translatePixelsToMatrix(this.canvas.width,
                                        this.canvas.height);

    var startRow = pos_TL.row;
    var startCol = pos_TR.col;
    var rowCount = pos_BR.row + 1;
    var colCount = pos_BL.col + 1;

    startRow = (startRow < 0) ? 0 : startRow;
    startCol = (startCol < 0) ? 0 : startCol;

    rowCount = (rowCount > this.grid.width) ? this.grid.width : rowCount;
    colCount = (colCount > this.grid.height) ? this.grid.height : colCount;

    var tileHeight = this.tile.height * this.zoomHelper.level;
    var tileWidth = this.tile.width * this.zoomHelper.level;

    for (var row = startRow; row < rowCount; row++) {
        for (var col = startCol; col < colCount; col++) {
            var xpos = (row - col) * tileHeight + (this.grid.width *
            this.zoomHelper.level);
```

```
            xpos += (this.canvas.width / 2) - ((tileWidth / 2) *
        this.zoomHelper.level) + this.scrollPosition.x;

            var ypos = (row + col) * (tileHeight / 2) + (this.grid.height *
        this.zoomHelper.level) + this.scrollPosition.y;

        if (this.tileMap[row] != null && this.tileMap[row][col] != null) {
            // Place building
        } else {
            if (Math.round(xpos) + tileWidth >= srcX &&
                Math.round(ypos) + tileHeight >= srcY &&
                Math.round(xpos) <= destX &&
                Math.round(ypos) <= destY) {


                this.c.drawImage(this.tile,
                            Math.round(xpos),
                            Math.round(ypos),
                            tileWidth,
                            tileHeight);

            }
        }

    }
  }
}

Game.prototype.zoomIn = function() {
    switch(this.zoomHelper.level) {
        case this.zoomHelper.NORMAL:
            this.zoomHelper.level = this.zoomHelper.CLOSE;
            break;
        case this.zoomHelper.FAR:
            this.zoomHelper.level = this.zoomHelper.NORMAL;
            break;
        case this.zoomHelper.CLOSE:
            return;
    }

    // Center the view
    this.scrollPosition.y -= (this.grid.height * this.zoomHelper.level) +
this.scrollPosition.y;
    this.scrollPosition.x -= (this.grid.width * this.zoomHelper.level) +
this.scrollPosition.x;
}

Game.prototype.zoomOut = function() {
    switch(this.zoomHelper.level) {
        case this.zoomHelper.NORMAL:
            this.zoomHelper.level = this.zoomHelper.FAR;
            break;
        case this.zoomHelper.CLOSE:
            this.zoomHelper.level = this.zoomHelper.NORMAL;
            break;
```

```
            case this.zoomHelper.FAR:
                return;
    }

    // Center the view
    this.scrollPosition.y -= (this.grid.height * this.zoomHelper.level) +
this.scrollPosition.y;
    this.scrollPosition.x -= (this.grid.width * this.zoomHelper.level) +
this.scrollPosition.x;
}

Game.prototype.rotateGrid = function(mW, mH, sW, sH) {
    var m = [];

    mW = (mW === undefined) ? this.grid.width : mW;
    mH = (mH === undefined) ? this.grid.height : mH;

    sW = (sW === undefined) ? 0 : sW;
    sH = (sH === undefined) ? 0 : sH;

    for (var i = sW; i < mW; i++) {
        for (var j = sH; j < mH; j++) {
            var row = (mW - j) - 1;

            if (this.tileMap[row] !== undefined && this.tileMap[row][i]) {
                m[i] = (m[i] === undefined) ? [] : m[i];
                m[i][j] = this.tileMap[row][i];
            }
        }
    }

    this.tileMap = m;
}
```

CHAPTER 4

HTML5 Sound and Processing Optimization

HTML5 brings game designers much more than the `canvas` element. Native support for sound (and video) is one key piece, letting you write games for which you manage sound in the same JavaScript environment as the graphics. Other pieces improve your JavaScript, whether breaking up tasks with Web Workers or letting you keep information on the player's device with local and session storage.

Adding Sound with the Audio Element

Previous versions of the HTML spec supported three ways of listening to an audio file in our page. We could:

- Use the `object` or `embed` tags to embed a file or a plugin such as LiveAudio (Netscape Navigator) or an ActiveMovie Control (Internet Explorer). As time went by, other plugins started to enter the market, such as Macromedia Flash (now Adobe Flash), REAL Player, or Apple's QuickTime, among others. To embed a MIDI or WAV file, we could either use `<embed src="music.mid" autostart="true" loop="true">` or embed a proprietary third-party plugin such as the Macromedia Flash Player and play the sound through our SWF file.

- Insert a Java Applet and play the sound through it.

- Add the `bgsound` attribute to the `body` element of the page (Internet Explorer only).

Browsers used to include varying sets of plugins, which meant that our sounds might play in one browser but not on another, even if both were installed on the same computer.

Luckily, with the advent of HTML5, we also gained the ability to play audio and video files natively through the use of the `<audio>` and `<video>` tags.

Unfortunately, the technological limitations in previous versions of HTML have been replaced by legal limitations in HTML5. Audio (and video) is encoded or decoded with the use of codecs, which are small software libraries that lets us encode/decode an audio or video data file or stream implementing a particular algorithm. Some algorithms are optimized for speed; other algorithms are optimized for lossless quality; just like conventional software, some of them are royalty-free and open and others are licensed.

In the case of "open" codecs, some companies such as Apple and Microsoft worry that they might be infringing a patent, which could make them liable in the case of a lawsuit—this is why they don't support them in their browsers. The opposite scenario is that other companies, such as the Mozilla Foundation or Opera Software, haven't made the necessary arrangements needed in order to use some licensed codecs yet.

Figure 4-1 shows which audio codecs are supported by each browser.

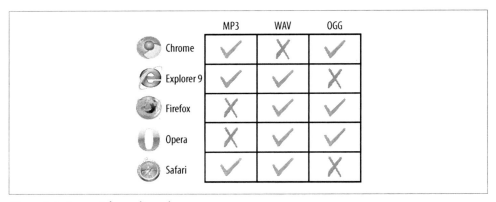

Figure 4-1. Support for audio codecs

Hopefully, by the time the HTML5 spec is finished, all browser vendors will have agreed to use a generic codec that works across all platforms. In the meantime, the W3C provides an elegant way of handling these sorts of problems with the ability to define "fallback audio sources."

To embed an audio player, all we need to do is to create an audio tag:

```
<audio src="../sounds/song.ogg" type="audio/ogg" controls />
```

which would show an audio player with a play/pause control (thanks to the control attribute's presence). If we press the "Play" button, it will attempt to play the sound identified by the src attribute. However, we may find ourselves using a browser that doesn't support that particular file format/codec, in which case we can do this:

```
<audio controls>
  <source src="../sounds/song.mp3" type="audio/mpeg">
  <source src="../sounds/song.ogg" type="audio/ogg">
</audio>
```

Instead of defining a single `src` parameter, the HTML5 `audio` tag allows us to define multiple audio files. If *song.mp3* can't be played for some reason, the browser will attempt to play the alternative *song.ogg*. If we had more sources, it would try to play every single one on the list until all of them failed or one of them worked. In addition to the `control` attribute, the HTML5 `audio` tag also supports other optional attributes:

loop

> Lets us loop the media file specified in the src attribute or in a source tag

autoplay

> Starts playing the sound as soon as it finishes loading the source

preload

> Lets us define our source preload strategy:
>
> *preload="none"*
>
> > Doesn't preload the file, which will be loaded when the user presses the play button
>
> *preload="metadata"*
>
> > Preloads only the metadata of the file
>
> *preload="auto"*
>
> > Lets the browser handle the preload of the file (which usually means to preload the entire file)

Of course, we can also create and use an HTML5 `audio` object using JavaScript instead of including an `audio` element in the document, as shown in Example 4-1.

Example 4-1. Creating HTML5 audio with JavaScript

```
<!DOCTYPE html>
<html lang="en">
  <head>
    <meta charset="UTF-8" />
    <title>Example 15 (HTML5 Audio)</title>
    <script>
      window.onload = function() {

        // Define an array with the audio files to try
        var sources = [
          ["../sounds/song.mp3", "audio/mpeg"],
          ["../sounds/song.ogg", "audio/ogg"]
        ];

        // Create the HTML5 Audio tag
        var audio = document.createElement('audio');

        // Cycle the "sources" array
        for (var i = 0; i < sources.length; i++) {

          // Later, you will learn how to check if a browser supports a given type
```

```
            // Create a source parameter
            var src = document.createElement('source');
            // Add both src and type attributes
            src.setAttribute("src", sources[i][0]);
            src.setAttribute("type", sources[i][1]);

            // Append the source to the Audio tag
            audio.appendChild(src);
        }

        // Attempt to play the sound
        audio.play();

    }
  </script>
  </head>
  <body>
    HTML5 Audio tag example.
  </body>
</html>
```

 The code repository also contains a more efficient example, *ex15-au-dioPlayer-alt.html*, with an alternative way of figuring out if the audio format is supported by the browser.

Along with the HTML5 Audio and Video objects, modern browsers trigger a new set of events called Media Events; a complete list is available at *https://developer.mozilla .org/En/Using_audio_and_video_in_Firefox*.

Some of the events that we will be using in this book and in our game are:

canplaythrough
> Triggered when the file download has almost finished and can be played in its entirety

playing
> Informs us if a sound is being played

ended
> Triggered when playback has finished

Playback of HTML5 audio (and video) files is controlled using the following methods and variables:

play()
> Plays the media.

pause()
> Pauses the media.

`currentTime`

Allows us to get or set the current playback time, expressed in milliseconds.

`Volume`

Allows us to get or set the current volume, as a value ranging from 0.0 to 1.0.

 An ongoing project in the Mozilla Foundation called the Audio Data API allows developers to create and manipulate sounds with better accuracy and a greater degree of control. (At the time of writing of this book, the API is available only in Firefox and in the latest versions of Chromium.) For more information, see *https://wiki.mozilla.org/Audio _Data_API*.

Now that you understand the basics on how to use this technology and its capabilities, you should also be aware of its limitations:

- Once you create an HTML5 `audio` object and start playing a sound, you can play that sound only once at a time. If you want to play the same sound two times simultaneously, you need an additional HTML5 `audio` object.

- There's a limit to the number of simultaneous playbacks; this limit varies from platform to platform. If you exceed that limit, you may experience errors that also vary from platform to platform.

A good rule of thumb is to keep the number of simultaneous audio playbacks to three (or fewer), as that is the playback limit on mobile OSs. Other platforms (such as Firefox running in a PC) can support a larger number of simultaneous playbacks.

When discussing the HTML Canvas section, we combined several images in a single image (called a sprite sheet) to optimize the number of requests made to the server, and then we could reference a particular image inside the sprite sheet by showing the rectangle of X1, Y1 and X2, Y2 (where X1, Y1, X2, Y2 are pixel coordinates). We can use a similar technique with sounds by combining them into a single file (called a *sound sheet*)—and instead of using pixel coordinates, we need to use time coordinates. (If you are feeling fancy, you could also put different sounds in the left and right audio channels, which could help you optimize requests even more, at the expense of losing one channel and playing sounds in mono.)

In our game, we're going to be using a utility called `SoundUtil` that will handle sound sheets and take care of maintaining a pool of audio objects for effective memory and resource management.

`SoundUtil` uses a different approach than the one used in Example 7. Instead of creating an HTML5 `audio` *tag*, it creates HTML5 `audio` *objects*. When you request the utility to play a sound, you pass some parameters:

- An array containing the files themselves and the format in which each file is encoded
- A start time, expressed in seconds
- An end time, expressed in milliseconds
- A volume value
- A boolean indicating whether you want the sound to loop forever, in which case, it will only respect the start time the first time it plays and won't respect the value passed as the end time

The play() method will call another method, getAudioObject(), that maintains a pool of audio objects available for reuse and keeps track of the maximum number of simultaneous playbacks. If no objects are available on the pool, it will automatically generate one unless the number of objects on the pool is equal to the maximum number of simultaneous playbacks, in which case it will return a null value and no sound will be played.

Once a sound finishes playing, we need to "free" the audio object to put it back in the pool of available audio objects by calling the freeAudioObject() method.

The entire utility can be seen in Example 4-2.

Example 4-2. SoundUtil.js

```
// Maximum number of sound objects allowed in the pool
var MAX_PLAYBACKS = 6;
var globalVolume = 0.6;

function SoundUtil(maxPlaybacks) {
  this.maxPlaybacks = maxPlaybacks;
  this.audioObjects = []; // Pool of audio objects available for reutilization
}

SoundUtil.prototype.play = function(file, startTime, duration, volume, loop) {

  // Get an audio object from pool
  var audioObject = this.getAudioObject();
  var suObj = this;

  /**
   * No audio objects are available on the pool. Don't play anything.
   * NOTE: This is the approach taken by toy organs; alternatively you
   * could also add objects into a queue to be played later on
   */
  if (audioObject !== null) {
    audioObject.obj.loop = loop;
    audioObject.obj.volume = volume;

    for (var i = 0; i < file.length; i++) {
      if (audioObject.obj.canPlayType(file[i][1]) === "maybe" ||
        audioObject.obj.canPlayType(file[i][1]) === "probably") {
        audioObject.obj.src = file[i][0];
```

```
        audioObject.obj.type = file[i][1];
        break;
      }
    }

    var playBack = function() {
      // Remove the event listener, otherwise it will
      // keep getting called over and over agian
      audioObject.obj.removeEventListener('canplaythrough', playBack, false);
      audioObject.obj.currentTime = startTime;
      audioObject.obj.play();

      // There's no need to listen if the object has finished
      // playing if it's playing in loop mode
      if (!loop) {
        setTimeout(function() {
          audioObject.obj.pause();
          suObj.freeAudioObject(audioObject);
        }, duration);
      }
    }

    audioObject.obj.addEventListener('canplaythrough', playBack, false);
  }
}

SoundUtil.prototype.getAudioObject = function() {
  if (this.audioObjects.length === 0) {
    var a = new Audio();
    var audioObject = {
      id: 0,
      obj: a,
      busy: true
    }

    this.audioObjects.push (audioObject);

    return audioObject;
  } else {
    for (var i = 0; i < this.audioObjects.length; i++) {
      if (!this.audioObjects[i].busy) {
        this.audioObjects[i].busy = true;
        return this.audioObjects[i];
      }
    }

    // No audio objects are free. Can we create a new one?
    if (this.audioObjects.length <= this.maxPlaybacks) {
      var a = new Audio();
      var audioObject = {
        id: this.audioObjects.length,
        obj: a,
        busy: true
      }
```

```
            this.audioObjects.push (audioObject);

            return audioObject;
        } else {
            return null;
        }
    }
  }
}

SoundUtil.prototype.freeAudioObject = function(audioObject) {
    for (var i = 0; i < this.audioObjects.length; i++) {
        if (this.audioObjects[i].id === audioObject.id) {
            this.audioObjects[i].currentTime = 0;
            this.audioObjects[i].busy = false;
        }
    }
}
```

To demonstrate how to use *SoundUtil*, we're going to combine it with the very first example shown in this book: the title screen. Example 4-3, *ex16-soundUtil.html*, is in the *examples* folder of the code repository included with this book.

Example 4-3. Adding sounds to our title screen

```
<!DOCTYPE html>
<html lang="en">
  <head>
    <meta charset="UTF-8" />
    <title>Example 16 - Title Screen with Sound</title>

    <!-- We're included the soundutil as an external file -->
    <script src="soundutil.js" charset="utf-8"></script>
    <script>

      window.onload = function () {
        var su = null;
        var sources = [
          ["../sounds/title.mp3", "audio/mp3"],
          ["../sounds/title.ogg", "audio/ogg"]
        ];

        var canvas = document.getElementById('myCanvas');
        var c = canvas.getContext('2d');

        var State = {
          _current: 0,
          INTRO: 0,
          LOADING: 1,
          LOADED: 2
        }

        window.addEventListener('click', handleClick, false);
        window.addEventListener('resize', doResize, false);

        doResize();
```

```javascript
// Check if the current browser supports playing MP3 or OGG files
if (soundIsSupported()) {
  // Play the title screen music
  playTitleMusic();
}

function playTitleMusic() {
  if (su) {
    su.play(sources, 0, 156000, globalVolume, false);
  }
}

function soundIsSupported() {
  var a = new Audio();
  var failures = 0;

  for (var i = 0; i < sources.length; i++) {
    if (a.canPlayType(sources[i][1]) !== "maybe" &&
        a.canPlayType(sources[i][1]) !== "probably") {
      failures++;
    }
  }

  if (failures !== sources.length) {
    su = new SoundUtil()
    return true;
  } else {
    return false;
  }
}

function handleClick() {
  if (State._current !== State.LOADING) {
    State._current = State.LOADING;
    fadeToWhite();
  }
}

function doResize() {
  canvas.width = document.body.clientWidth;
  canvas.height = document.body.clientHeight;

  switch (State._current) {
    case State.INTRO:
      showIntro ();
      break;
  }
}

function fadeToWhite(alphaVal) {
  // If the function hasn't received any parameters, start with 0.02
  var alphaVal = (alphaVal == undefined) ? 0.02 : parseFloat(alphaVal) + 0.02;
```

```
      // Set the color to white
      c.fillStyle = '#FFFFFF';
      // Set the Global Alpha
      c.globalAlpha = alphaVal;

      // Make a rectangle as big as the canvas
      c.fillRect(0, 0, canvas.width, canvas.height);

      if (alphaVal < 1.0) {
        setTimeout(function() {
          fadeToWhite(alphaVal);
        }, 30);
      } else {
        State._current = State.LOADED;
      }
    }

function showIntro () {
    var phrase = "Click or tap the screen to start the game";

    // Clear the canvas
    c.clearRect (0, 0, canvas.width, canvas.height);

    // Make a nice blue gradient
    var grd = c.createLinearGradient(0, canvas.height, canvas.width, 0);
    grd.addColorStop(0, '#ceefff');
    grd.addColorStop(1, '#52bcff');

    c.fillStyle = grd;
    c.fillRect(0, 0, canvas.width, canvas.height);

    var logoImg = new Image();
    logoImg.src = '../img/logo.png';

    // Store the original width value so that we can
    // keep the same width/height ratio later
    var originalWidth = logoImg.width;

    // Compute the new width and height values
    logoImg.width = Math.round((50 * document.body.clientWidth) / 100);
    logoImg.height = Math.round((logoImg.width * logoImg.height) /
originalWidth);

    // Create an small utility object
    var logo = {
      img: logoImg,
      x: (canvas.width/2) - (logoImg.width/2),
      y: (canvas.height/2) - (logoImg.height/2)
    }

    // Present the image
    c.drawImage(logo.img, logo.x, logo.y, logo.img.width, logo.img.height);
```

```
        // Change the color to black
        c.fillStyle = '#000000';
        c.font = 'bold 16px Arial, sans-serif';

        var textSize = c.measureText (phrase);
        var xCoord = (canvas.width / 2) - (textSize.width / 2);

        c.fillText (phrase, xCoord, (logo.y + logo.img.height) + 50);
      }
    }
  </script>
  <style type="text/css" media="screen">
    html { height: 100%; overflow: hidden }
    body {
      margin: 0px;
      padding: 0px;
      height: 100%;
    }
  </style>

</head>
<body>
  <canvas id="myCanvas" width="100" height="100">
    Your browser doesn't include support for the canvas tag.
  </canvas>
</body>
</html>
```

We're also going to modify *ex14-gui.html* to add a background music to our game. The example can be found online as *ex14-gui-sound.html*.

Managing Computationally Expensive Work with the Web Workers API

Now that we have managed to develop a high-performance graphics rendering function for our final game, it would be nice to implement a path-finding function, which will be useful to build roads or to display characters going from point A to point B.

In a nutshell, path-finding algorithms discover the shortest route between two points in an *n*-dimensional space, usually 2D or 3D.

Usually, path finding is one of the few areas that only a few selected people can get right—and that many people (hopefully not including us) will get wrong. It is one of the most expensive processes to execute, and the most efficient solution usually requires us to modify the algorithm to customize it to our product.

One of the best algorithms to handle path finding is A*, which is a variation of Dijkstra's algorithm. The problem with any path-finding algorithm—or, for that matter, any computationally expensive operation that needs more than a couple of milliseconds to get solved—is that in JavaScript, they produce an effect called "interface locking" in which the browser freezes until the operation has finished.

Fortunately, the HTML5 specification also provides a new API called Web Workers. Web Workers (usually just called "workers") allow us to execute relatively computational expensive and long-lived scripts in the background without affecting the main user interface of the browser.

 Workers are not silver bullets that will magically help us to solve tasks that are eating 100% of our CPU processing capabilities. If a task is processor-intensive using the conventional approach, it will probably also be processor-intensive when using workers and will wind up affecting the user experience anyway. However, if a task is consuming 30% of the CPU, workers can help us minimize the impact on the user interface by executing the task in parallel.

Also, there are some limitations:

- Because each worker runs in a totally separate, thread-safe context from the page that executed it (also known as a sandbox), they won't have access to the DOM and `window` objects.

- Although you can spawn new workers from within a worker (this feature is not available in Google Chrome), be careful, because this approach can lead to bugs that are very difficult to debug.

Workers can be created with this code:

```
var worker = new Worker(PATH_TO_A_JS_SCRIPT);
```

where *PATH_TO_A_JS_SCRIPT* could be, for example, *astar.js*. Once our worker has been created, we can terminate the execution at any given time by calling `worker.close()`. If a worker has been closed and we need to perform a new operation, we'll need to create a new worker object.

Back and forth communication with Web Workers is accomplished by using the `worker.postMessage(object)` method to send a message and defining a callback function on the `worker.onmessage` event. Additionally, you can define an `onerror` handler to process errors on the worker.

Just like a conventional page, Web Workers also allow us to call external scripts by using the function *importScripts()*. This function accepts zero or multiple parameters (each parameter is a JavaScript file).

An example implementation of the A* algorithm in JavaScript called using Web Workers can be found in the code repository as *ex17-grid-astar.html*. Figure 4-2 shows that worker's progress. The code is shown in Example 17 and an A* implementation developed in JavaScript.

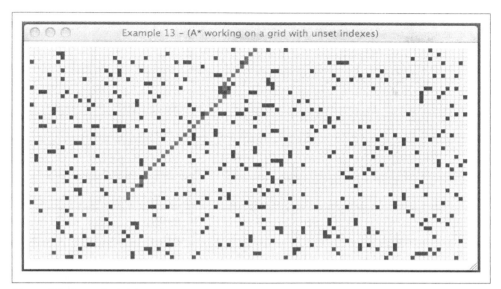
Figure 4-2. Example 4-4 in action

Example 4-4. Path-finding HTML

```
<!DOCTYPE html>
<html lang="en">
  <head>
    <meta charset="UTF-8" />
    <title>Example 17 - (A* working on a grid with unset indexes using
          web workers)</title>

    <script>

      window.onload = function () {
        var tileMap = [];

        var path = {
          start: null,
          stop: null
        }

        var tile = {
          width: 6,
          height: 6
        }

        var grid = {
          width: 100,
          height: 100
        }

        var canvas = document.getElementById('myCanvas');
        canvas.addEventListener('click', handleClick, false);
```

```
var c = canvas.getContext('2d');

// Generate 1000 random elements
for (var i = 0; i < 1000; i++) {
  generateRandomElement();
}

// Draw the entire grid
draw();

function handleClick(e) {
  // When a click is detected, translate the mouse
  // coordinates to pixel coordinates
  var row = Math.floor((e.clientX - 10) / tile.width);
  var column = Math.floor((e.clientY - 10) / tile.height);

  if (tileMap[row] == null) {
    tileMap[row] = [];
  }

  if (tileMap[row][column] !== 0 && tileMap[row][column] !== 1) {
    tileMap[row][column] = 0;

    if (path.start === null) {
      path.start = {x: row, y: column};
    } else {
      path.stop = {x: row, y: column};

      callWorker(path, processWorkerResults);

      path.start = null;
      path.stop = null;
    }

    draw();
  }
}

function callWorker(path, callback) {
  var w = new Worker('astar.js');
  w.postMessage({
    tileMap: tileMap,
    grid: {
      width: grid.width,
      height: grid.height
    },
    start: path.start,
    stop: path.stop
  });
  w.onmessage = callback;
}

function processWorkerResults(e) {
  if (e.data.length > 0) {
```

```
    for (var i = 0, len = e.data.length; i < len; i++) {
      if (tileMap[e.data[i].x] === undefined) {
        tileMap[e.data[i].x] = [];
      }

      tileMap[e.data[i].x][e.data[i].y] = 0;
    }
  }

  draw();
}

function generateRandomElement() {
  var rndRow = Math.floor(Math.random() * (grid.width + 1));
  var rndCol = Math.floor(Math.random() * (grid.height + 1));


  if (tileMap[rndRow] == null) {
    tileMap[rndRow] = [];
  }
  tileMap[rndRow][rndCol] = 1;
}

function draw(srcX, srcY, destX, destY) {
  srcX = (srcX === undefined) ? 0 : srcX;
  srcY = (srcY === undefined) ? 0 : srcY;
  destX = (destX === undefined) ? canvas.width : destX;
  destY = (destY === undefined) ? canvas.height : destY;

  c.fillStyle = '#FFFFFF';
  c.fillRect (srcX, srcY, destX + 1, destY + 1);
  c.fillStyle = '#000000';

  var startRow = 0;
  var startCol = 0;
  var rowCount = startRow + Math.floor(canvas.width / tile.width) + 1;
  var colCount = startCol + Math.floor(canvas.height / tile.height) + 1;

  rowCount = ((startRow + rowCount) > grid.width) ? grid.width : rowCount;
  colCount = ((startCol + colCount) > grid.height) ? grid.height : colCount;

  for (var row = startRow; row < rowCount; row++) {
    for (var col = startCol; col < colCount; col++) {
      var tilePositionX = tile.width * row;
      var tilePositionY = tile.height * col;

      if (tilePositionX >= srcX && tilePositionY >= srcY &&
        tilePositionX <= (srcX + destX) &&
        tilePositionY <= (srcY + destY)) {

        if (tileMap[row] != null && tileMap[row][col] != null) {
          if (tileMap[row][col] == 0) {
            c.fillStyle = '#CC0000';
          } else {
            c.fillStyle = '#0000FF';
```

```
                }
              c.fillRect(tilePositionX, tilePositionY, tile.width, tile.height);
            } else {
              c.strokeStyle = '#CCCCCC';
              c.strokeRect(tilePositionX, tilePositionY, tile.width, tile.height);
            }
          }
        }
      }
    }
  }
  </script>
  </head>
  <body>
  <canvas id="myCanvas" width="600" height="300"></canvas>
  <br />

  </body>
</html>
```

Example 4-5. JavaScript A class*

```
// The worker will take care of the instantiation of the astar class
onmessage = function(e){
  var a = new aStar(e.data.tileMap, e.data.grid.width, e.data.grid.height, e.data.start,
e.data.stop);
  postMessage(a);
}


// A* path-finding class adjusted for a tileMap with noncontiguous indexes

/**
 * @param tileMap: A 2-dimensional matrix with noncontiguous indexes
 * @param gridW: Grid width measured in rows
 * @param gridH: Grid height measured in columns
 * @param src: Source point, an object containing X and Y
 *              coordinates representing row/column
 * @param dest: Destination point, an object containing
 *               X and Y coordinates representing row/column
 * @param createPositions: [OPTIONAL] A boolean indicating whether
 *                          traversing through the tileMap should
 *                          create new indexes (default TRUE)
 */
var aStar = function(tileMap, gridW, gridH, src, dest, createPositions) {
  this.openList = new NodeList(true, 'F');
  this.closedList = new NodeList();
  this.path = new NodeList();
  this.src = src;
  this.dest = dest;
  this.createPositions = (createPositions === undefined) ? true : createPositions;
  this.currentNode = null;

  var grid = {
    rows: gridW,
```

```
  cols: gridH
}

this.openList.add(new Node(null, this.src));

while (!this.openList.isEmpty()) {
  this.currentNode = this.openList.get(0);
  this.currentNode.visited = true;

  if (this.checkDifference(this.currentNode, this.dest)) {
    // Destination reached :)
    break;
  }

  this.closedList.add(this.currentNode);
  this.openList.remove(0);

  // Check the 8 neighbors around this node
  var nstart = {
    x: (((this.currentNode.x - 1) >= 0) ? this.currentNode.x - 1 : 0),
    y: (((this.currentNode.y - 1) >= 0) ? this.currentNode.y - 1 : 0),
  }

  var nstop = {
    x: (((this.currentNode.x + 1) <= grid.rows) ? this.currentNode.x + 1 : grid.rows),
    y: (((this.currentNode.y + 1) <= grid.cols) ? this.currentNode.y + 1 : grid.cols),
  }

  for (var row = nstart.x; row <= nstop.x; row++) {
    for (var col = nstart.y; col <= nstop.y; col++) {

      // The row is not available on the original tileMap, should we keep going?
      if (tileMap[row] === undefined) {
        if (!this.createPositions) {
          continue;
        }
      }

      // Check for buildings or other obstructions
      if (tileMap[row] !== undefined && tileMap[row][col] === 1) {
        continue;
      }

      var element = this.closedList.getByXY(row, col);
      if (element !== null) {
        // this element is already on the closed list
        continue;
      } else {
        element = this.openList.getByXY(row, col);
        if (element !== null) {
          // this element is already on the closed list
          continue;
        }
      }
```

```
          // Not present in any of the lists, keep going.
          var n = new Node(this.currentNode, {x: row, y: col});
          n.G = this.currentNode.G + 1;
          n.H = this.getDistance(this.currentNode, n);
          n.F = n.G + n.H;

          this.openList.add(n);
        }
      }
    }
  }

  while (this.currentNode.parentNode !== null) {
    this.path.add(this.currentNode);
    this.currentNode = this.currentNode.parentNode;
  }

  return this.path.list;
}

aStar.prototype.checkDifference = function(src, dest) {
  return (src.x === dest.x && src.y === dest.y);
}

aStar.prototype.getDistance = function(src, dest) {
  return Math.abs(src.x - dest.x) + Math.abs(src.y - dest.y);
}

function Node(parentNode, src) {
  this.parentNode = parentNode;
    this.x = src.x;
    this.y = src.y;
    this.F = 0;
    this.G = 0;
    this.H = 0;
}

var NodeList = function(sorted, sortParam) {
  this.sort = (sorted === undefined) ? false : sorted;
  this.sortParam = (sortParam === undefined) ? 'F' : sortParam;
  this.list = [];
  this.coordMatrix = [];
}

NodeList.prototype.add = function(element) {
  this.list.push(element);

  if (this.coordMatrix[element.x] === undefined) {
    this.coordMatrix[element.x] = [];
  }

  this.coordMatrix[element.x][element.y] = element;

  if (this.sort) {
    var sortBy = this.sortParam;
    this.list.sort(function(o1, o2) { return o1[sortBy] - o2[sortBy]; });
```

```
    }
  }

NodeList.prototype.remove = function(pos) {
  this.list.splice(pos, 1);
}

NodeList.prototype.get = function(pos) {
  return this.list[pos];
}

NodeList.prototype.size = function() {
  return this.list.length;
}

NodeList.prototype.isEmpty = function() {
  return (this.list.length == 0);
}

NodeList.prototype.getByXY = function(x, y) {
  if (this.coordMatrix[x] === undefined) {
    return null;
  } else {
    var obj = this.coordMatrix[x][y];

    if (obj == undefined) {
      return null;
    } else {
      return obj;
    }
  }
}
NodeList.prototype.print = function() {
  for (var i = 0, len = this.list.length; i < len; i++) {
    console.log(this.list[i].x + ' ' + this.list[i].y);
  }
}
```

Local Storage and Session Storage

One limitation that web developers had to deal with in the past was that the size of cookies wasn't enough to save anything too big or important; it was limited to just 4K. Nowadays, modern web browsers are including support for Web Storage, a tool that can help us save *at least* 5 megabytes (MB) on the user's local HDD (hard disk drive). However, when we say "at least 5 MB," it can actually be more or less than that amount, depending on which browser we're using, and—in some cases (as in Opera)—the space quota that we defined in our settings panel. In some cases, the Web Storage capabilities could be disabled entirely. If we exceed the 5 MB of storage, the browser will throw a QUOTA_EXCEEDED_ERR exception, so it's very important to surround calls to local Storage or sessionStorage in a try-catch block and—just like we should be doing with the rest of our code—handle any exceptions appropriately.

Expect Web Storage to behave very similarly to cookies:

- The functionality could be disabled.
- We have a maximum amount of elements that we can store—4K in the case of cookies and 5MB in the case of Web Storage, but it could be less than that as well.
- Users can delete or manually create and/or modify the contents of our storage folder at any given time.
- Browsers can also decide to automatically "expire" the content of our storage folder.
- The quota is given per domain name, and shared by all the subdomains (i.e., *site1.example.com*, *site2.example.com*, and *site3.example.com* share the same folder).

However, Web Storage differs from cookies in the following ways:

- The data saved with the Web Storage API can only be queries made by the client, not by the server.
- The contents do not travel "back and forth" on every request.
- With the exception of `sessionStorage` (which deletes its contents once the session is over), we can't explicitly specify an expiration date.
- Just as with cookies, it's best to *not* use Web Storage to save anything important.

Other than that, it's a great tool that can help us do things that we couldn't do before, like caching objects to increase loading performance the next time the user opens our application, saving a draft of the document we're working on, or even using it as a virtual memory container.

Once you understand the limitations and capabilities of Web Storage, the rest is pretty straightforward:

- Data is stored in an array of key-value pairs that are treated and stored like strings.
- The difference between `localStorage` and `sessionStorage` is that `localStorage` stores the data permanently (or until the user or the browser decides to dispose of it), and `sessionStorage` stores it only for the duration of the "session" (until we close the tab/window).

The Web Storage API consists of only four methods:

`localStorage.setItem(key, value)`
    Adds an item

`localStorage.getItem(key)`
    Queries an existing item

`localStorage.removeItem(key)`
    Removes a specific item

```
localStorage.clear()
```
Entirely deletes the contents of our *localStorage* folder

Example 4-6 shows how to use Web Storage.

Example 4-6. Using Web Storage

```
<!DOCTYPE html>
<html lang="en">
  <head>
    <meta charset="UTF-8" />
    <title>Canvas Example 18 (LocalStorage)</title>

    <script>
      window.onload = function () {
        var binMatrix = null;
        var matrixSize = 25;

        // This is the key name under which we will be storing,
        // loading or removing the data
        var KEY_NAME = "matrix";

        var matrix = document.getElementById('matrix');
        var load = document.getElementById('load');
        var save = document.getElementById('save');
        var clear = document.getElementById('clear');

        binMatrix = initializeMatrix(matrixSize);
        printMatrix(binMatrix, matrix);

        // Handle click events on the buttons
        load.addEventListener('click', handleLoad, false);
        save.addEventListener('click', handleSave, false);
        clear.addEventListener('click', handleClear, false);

        function handleLoad() {
          var m = localStorage.getItem(KEY_NAME);

          try {
            // If we haven't set the key yet, or we removed its
            // contents with the "m" variable,
            // will be null.
            if (m == null) {
              alert("You haven't stored a matrix yet.");
            } else {
              // Otherwise, we need to "parse" the contents back to an array.
              binMatrix = JSON.parse(m);

              // Clear the original matrix
              matrix.innerHTML = null;

              // And reprint it
              printMatrix(binMatrix, matrix);
            }
```

```
      } catch(e) {
        alert("The following error occurred while trying to load the matrix: " + e);
      }
    }

    function handleSave() {
      try {
        // Read the values of the checkbox inside the "matrix" div
        // and replace them accordingly in the array
        for (var i = 0; i < matrixSize; i++) {
          for (var j = 0; j < matrixSize; j++) {
            var pos = (i + j) + (i * matrixSize);

            if (matrix.childNodes[pos].tagName == "INPUT") {
              binMatrix[i][j] = (matrix.childNodes[pos].checked) ? 1 : 0;
            }
          }
        }
        // Finally, stringify the matrix for storage and save it
        localStorage.setItem(KEY_NAME, JSON.stringify(binMatrix));
      } catch(e) {
        alert("The following error occurred while trying to save the matrix: " + e);
      }
    }

    function handleClear() {
      if (confirm("Are you sure that you want to empty the matrix?")) {
        try {
          localStorage.removeItem(KEY_NAME);

          // Clear the original matrix
          matrix.innerHTML = null;
          binMatrix = null;

          // Regenerate the matrix
          binMatrix = initializeMatrix(matrixSize);

          // And reprint it
          printMatrix(binMatrix, matrix);
        } catch(e) {
          alert("The following error occurred while trying to remove the matrix: " + e);
        }
      }
    }
  }

/**
 * Generic matrix initialization routine
 */
function initializeMatrix(size) {
  var m = [];

  for (var i = 0; i < size; i++) {
    m[i] = [];
```

```javascript
      for (var j = 0; j < size; j++) {
        m[i][j] = 0;
      }
    }

    return m;
  }

  /**
   * The following function gets the matrix and converts it to a long string
   * of checkboxes, to then insert it inside the "matrix" <div>
   * It is considered a good practice, unless you really need to
   * do otherwise, to use strings to generate HTML elements
   * in order to avoid having to create a new object for every new
   * element that you want to add.
   * Concatenate all the strings together and insert them to the
   * object "all at once" in order to prevent
   * unnecessary and performance-heavy browser reflows.
   */
  function printMatrix(m, elem) {
    var str = "";

    for (var i = 0, x = m.length; i < x; i++) {
      for (var j = 0, r = m[i].length; j < r; j++) {
        str += '<input type="checkbox" class="' + i + ' - ' + j + '" ';
        str += (m[i][j] == 1) ? 'checked' : '';
        str += ' />';
        str += ((j + 1) == r) ? '<div class="clb"></div>' : '';
      }
    }

    elem.innerHTML = str;
  }
</script>

<style type="text/css" media="screen">
  body {
    margin: 20px;
    padding: 0px;
  }

  #matrix input {
    float: left;
    padding: 0px;
    margin: 0px;
  }
  div.clb { clear: both; }
</style>
</head>
<body>
  <input type="button" id="load" value="Load Matrix" />
  <input type="button" id="save" value="Save Matrix" />
  <input type="button" id="clear" value="Clear Matrix" />

  <br /><br />
```

```
    <div id="matrix"></div>
  </body>
</html>
```

The complete code for Example 4-6 is stored as *ex18-localStorage.html* in the *examples* folder of the code repository.

 For more information, refer to the Web Storage section of the HTML5 specification (still a draft at the time of writing of this book): *http://dev .w3.org/html5/webstorage/*.

We're not going to be using localStorage in our game. However, if you're working with very large grids full of elements, it's recommended to work only with "portions" of the matrix containing all of our objects. By slightly modifying the code presented here, you can download additional tile positions from a server as you scroll around the grid and leave them ready to be swapped with the current matrix by storing the result on localStorage.

CHAPTER 5

Connecting the Game to People

You've built an attractive game with interactive graphics and music. Now you just need to set things up to bring people in! That means putting logic on the server, keeping people from tinkering with your logic to break things (in their favor), and connecting your application to a place with a lot of people—Facebook!

Cheat Prevention and Server-Side Operations

One of the main issues when developing an online video game is cheat prevention. Just like in conventional web development, we can't trust any user, so securing our application against malicious users and handling unexpected inputs or return values should always be our highest priority.

The risk is even greater in open source games, particularly those built with web technologies such as JavaScript and HTML, in which one can tamper with variables (or even POST/GET requests) easily or even modify code on the client in real time on the fly.

Unfortunately, the solution to this problem varies from game to game, but it almost always relies on two important (and usually very inefficient) approaches that need to be solved in the predevelopment and development stages of game creation:

- Try to minimize the risk of committing fraud on the client by design
- Validate *everything* on the server

In the case of our game, and in most real-time social strategy games, these are some of the things we need to keep in mind:

- Every user should have her own account balance stored in a database field or table (depending on whether you want to keep track of individual transactions) and every purchase or sell operation should update the balance.
- We need to keep a Unix time value on the server and sync the value with the client regularly

- Perhaps the most important thing to keep in mind (and the most reliable anti-cheating method) is that we need to design the game in such a way as to reliably predict the user score at any given time *on the server* without ever interacting with the client.

How do we do that? Let's consider the following scenario:

Initially, the user has a balance of 2000 gold coins, 0 buildings, an account "creation time" of 1293861600 (which is the Unix timestamp for January 1, 2011, at 00:00:00) and a "last update" time of 1293861600 (same timestamp as the start time).

We have three possible structures that we can build:

- An ice cream shop that costs 250 gold coins and pays 5 gold coins every 30 minutes
- A hotel that costs 1,000 gold coins and pays 30 gold coins per hour
- A cinema that costs 500 gold coins and pays 12 gold coins every 30 minutes

The user builds an ice cream shop at 1293861660 (January 1, 2011, at 00:01:00, one minute after the account creation).

He then decides to build a hotel at 1294084800 (January 3, 2011, at 14:00:00).

At 1294120800 (January 4, 2011, at 00:00:00), the user builds a cinema.

At 1294639200 (January 10, 2011, at 00:00:00), he returns to the game and wants to see his account balance.

One approach to handle this situation would be to keep track of all the buildings that the user has purchased and to add a "last update" field in the user's account that knows the last time that he queried his account balance or purchased/sold a building. Then, every time that he wants to see his account balance or does a buy/sell operation, we would perform the following steps:

1. Update the "last update" field of the user with the current timestamp.
2. Start cycling through all the buildings that the user owns.
3. Calculate the time difference (in seconds) between the current time and the "last update" time of the user field.
4. Divide the result by the number of seconds of the payment fractions, and "floor" the result.
5. Multiply the result by the number of gold coins given on each fraction.
6. Update the account balance by adding up the result.
7. Depending on the operation that we are performing (show, build, or sell), either show the account balance or subtract/add the cost of the building.
8. If we are selling a building, delete the association.

If we apply this method to the example scenario described, we can deduce the following:

- On 1293861660, the user decided to build an ice cream shop. At the time, he had 0 other buildings, so we just need to update his account balance and his "last update" time and create an association. The "last update" time of this association will be 1293861660.

  The user's account balance will now be 1750 (2000 − 250).

- On 1294084800, he decided to build a hotel. Before we create a new association for the hotel, we need to recalculate his account balance. We know that he purchased the ice cream shop on 1293861660, so we update the "last update" field of the user to 1294084800; in order to know how much income the ice cream shop has created so far, we perform the following calculation:

  ```
  timeDiff = 1294084800 - 1293861660 = 223140 seconds
  ```

  Ice cream shops generate a profit of 5 gold coins every 30 minutes (1800 seconds), so we need to do this calculation:

  ```
  result = timeDiff / 1800 seconds = 123.97
  ```

  or just 123 once we floor the result:

  ```
  result = result * 5 = 615 gold coins
  ```

  We finally update the account balance to 1750 + 615 = 2365, create the association for the hotel (using 1294084800 as the "last update" time), and take away the cost of the hotel. The user's account balance will now be 1365 (2365 − 1000).

- On 1294120800, he purchased a cinema, so we perform the same steps as before (this time for two buildings, the ice cream shop and the hotel):

  ```
  timeDiff = 1294120800 - 1294084800 = 36000 seconds

  iceCreamShopResult = timeDiff / 1800 = 20

  iceCreamShopResult = iceCreamShopResult * 5 gold coins = 100 gold coins

  hotelResult = timeDiff / 3600 seconds (one hour) = 10

  hotelResult = hotelResult * 30 gold coins = 300 gold coins

  accBalance = accBalance + hotelResult + iceCreamShopResult = 1765

  accBalance = accBalance - 500 gold coins (the cost of the parking lot)
  ```

  The user's account balance at this point will be 1265.

- Finally, on 1294639200, he wants to check his account balance once again:

  ```
  timeDiff = 1294639200 - 1294120800 = 518400 seconds

  iceCreamShopResult = timeDiff / 1800 = 288

  iceCreamShopResult = iceCreamShopResult * 5 = 1440 gold coins
  ```

```
hotelResult = timeDiff / 3600 seconds (one hour) = 144

hotelResult = hotelResult * 30 = 4320 gold coins

cinemaResult = timeDiff / 1800 = 288

cinemaResult = cinemaResult * 12 = 3456 gold coins

accBalance = accBalance + cinemaResult + hotelResult + iceCreamShopResult
```

This means that, by January 10, 2011, at 00:00:00, we can confidently predict that the user's account balance will be 10481.

Although it will be extremely difficult, if not impossible, to prevent the user from modifying the client side of our game, using the method explained here, we can certainly prevent malicious users from gaining an unfair advantage to other players, as the modifications that they make affect them only locally, not on the server. Another useful feature that could be added to this idea is a concept used by Zynga in some of their games, which is that instead of generating profit constantly—as in this case—the user must "collect" the profit generated by the building. For example, if a building generates 500 coins every 30 minutes and the user didn't play for 3 days, when he collects the money, he'll be awarded just 500 coins. All that we need to do to implement this approach is to check whether the result of the time difference is greater than the profit generated by the building; if so, a flag should be set to true. Then the user will need to manually "collect" the money, resetting the flag to false.

We can implement the original method explained previously using the data model shown in Figure 5-1.

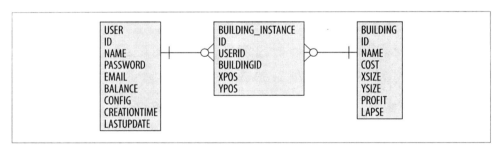

Figure 5-1. Data model connecting users and buildings

The data model presented in Figure 5-1 tells us that:

Any user can be associated to zero or many building instances.
Any individual instance must have one user.
Any building may also be associated to zero or many building instances.
Any building instances must be associated to one building.

For our game, we're going to implement this data model and the software that controls its behavior using MySQL and PHP:

- You can install and configure MySQL on your system; see *http://dev.mysql.com/ usingmysql/get_started.html*.
- You can install and configure PHP on your system; see *http://us.php.net/manual/ en/install.php*. In order to run PHP, you will also need to install a web server such as Apache, Lighttpd, or nginx. The instructions on how to install (and configure) each one can also be found at the above *.php* URL.

Once you have configured PHP and MySQL on your computer (including setting up a root password), you can connect to the server by opening a new terminal and executing the command:

```
mysql -hlocalhost -uroot -p<YOURPASSWORD>
```

If you haven't configured a password for the root user, try:

```
mysql -hlocalhost -uroot
```

Once you are connected, you should get access to the `mysql` prompt:

```
scarlet:~ andres$ mysql -uroot -hlocalhost
Welcome to the MySQL monitor.  Commands end with ; or \g.
Your MySQL connection id is 816
Server version: 5.1.45 MySQL Community Server (GPL)

Type 'help;' or '\h' for help. Type '\c' to clear the current input statement.

mysql>
```

 The MySQL Server version may differ on your system.

Now that we are connected to our database, let's create the database for our game by using the following command:

```
CREATE DATABASE mygame;
```

If everything went well, you should see the following output:

```
mysql> CREATE DATABASE mygame;
Query OK, 1 row affected (0.00 sec)
```

In order to create tables inside the *mygame* database, we first need to tell MySQL to select it as the active database:

```
USE mygame;
```

If no other errors occurred, you should see the following return value:

```
mysql> USE mygame;
Database changed
```

In the code repository folder called *server* at *https://github.com/andrespagella/Making -Isometric-Real-time-Games/tree/master/server* you will find two *.sql* files: *model-empty.sql* and *model-filled.sql*. Download *model-filled.sql* to your computer, and go back to the MySQL prompt. Using the download path of the file, execute the following statement:

```
source <PATH_TO_SQL_FILE>;
```

If everything went well, you should see the following output:

```
mysql> source /Users/andres/Desktop/model-filled.sql
Query OK, 0 rows affected (0.00 sec)

Query OK, 0 rows affected (0.00 sec)

Query OK, 0 rows affected (0.00 sec)

Query OK, 4 rows affected (0.05 sec)

Query OK, 0 rows affected (0.05 sec)

Query OK, 0 rows affected (0.07 sec)

Query OK, 0 rows affected (0.00 sec)

Query OK, 0 rows affected (0.10 sec)

Query OK, 0 rows affected (0.09 sec)

mysql>
```

The SQL file will generate three database tables: users, buildings, and building_ instances and will prefill the buildings table with four buildings (which we'll be using in the final game): an ice cream shop, a hotel, a cinema, and a tree.

In order to use the *mygame* database with our PHP scripts, we also need to generate a MySQL user, giving the user access to execute the SELECT, INSERT, UPDATE, and DELETE operations. We can do that by executing the following statements in the MySQL prompt:

```
CREATE USER 'mygameuser'@'localhost' IDENTIFIED BY 'game123';
GRANT SELECT, INSERT, UPDATE, DELETE ON mygame.* TO 'mygameuser'@'localhost';
```

As always, the output shouldn't display any errors:

```
mysql> CREATE USER 'mygameuser'@'localhost' IDENTIFIED BY 'game123';
Query OK, 0 rows affected (0.09 sec)

mysql> GRANT SELECT, INSERT, UPDATE, DELETE ON mygame.* TO 'mygameuser'@'localhost';
Query OK, 0 rows affected (0.07 sec)

mysql>
```

For more information on how to use MySQL, please refer to the official MySQL Developer portal at *http://dev.mysql.com*.

Inside the *server* folder of the GitHub repository, you will also find the following files and folders:

config.php
    That defines the database connection details as well as the size of the grid.

classes/class.dbutil.php
    A simple MySQL database utility class

classes/class.users.php
    Handles user-related operations

classes/class.buildings.php
    Handles building-related operations

classes/class.operations.php
    Takes care of the instantiation and retrieval of building instances

classes/class.user.php
    A user class

classes/class.building.php
    A building class

classes/class.buildingInstance.php
    A buildingInstance class

test-database.php
    A useful script that tries to connect to the database and tests whether it can store, retrieve, and remove entries

registration.php
    A script that shows you how to register a new user using the classes mentioned previously

authentication.php
    A script that shows you how to authenticate and initiate a user session using the classes listed previously

The Path to the Final Game

In the previous section, you learned how to implement the server scripts and database structure for our game. Now we're going to combine the game that we've developed so far and integrate it into our server-side scripts to handle registration, authentication, and populating values such as the ones in the "build" panel or the account balance with the real values stored in the database.

Our file and folder structure for the final game will look like this:

index.php
    Contains the index page; handles authentication and user registration.

game.php
    Contains the actual game. If the session is not active, the user will be bounced back to the index to authenticate or register. The code inside this file will be very similar to Example 3-1, but modified to display real values inside the containers and broken down into several JavaScript files for easier maintenance.

async/
    Contains the PHP scripts to handle asynchronous calls made with JavaScript using XMLHttpRequest (AJAX).

css/
    Contains the CSS files *site.css* (used in *index.php*) and *ui-style.css* (used in our game).

js/
    Contains all the JavaScript files used by our game.

Besides assigning "real" values to all the fields, *game.php* will perform an additional step to get all the Building Instances associated to the current user and will automatically populate the `tileMap` matrix with the buildings that the user has purchased. Additionally, for decorative purposes, the registration bit on *index.php* will also randomly create Building Instances of the "Tree" building (10% of the total size of the grid will be filled with trees).

The instantiation of those building instances in our grid is going to be performed by a function called `initializeGrid()` that combines the PHP array containing the building instances with the JavaScript `tileMap` matrix of our game. Unless the user manages to fill the entire grid with objects (which means that he'd need to buy 62,500 buildings, which is highly unlikely), this approach is enough for our needs. Another solution would have been to create an identical `tileMap` matrix in PHP, encode it to JSON, and then replace the original `tileMap` matrix (in the JavaScript) with the decoded JSON, but on my tests I found this approach to be too inefficient because decoding large JSON objects in JavaScript has a lot of overhead.

  If you want to use a bigger grid for your own personal or professional project, you might want to break down the initialization routine to load only a section of the entire grid and load the rest dynamically as you scroll. The reason why we're not implementing this approach in this case is because mobile devices have a (somewhat) good download bandwidth, but a terrible roundtrip/connection latency (especially when they are connected via 3G), meaning that it's generally best to download everything in a single batch rather than doing several "small" requests for additional data.

We're also going to modify our Game class a bit to prevent it from displaying the grid as soon as it is instantiated. The modification consists in removing the final two lines of the Game() constructor:

```
this.doResize()
this.draw()
```

Another thing that we're going to integrate at this point is a modification of our title screen example, to be shown as soon as the user loads the *game.php* page. Adding the title screen also means that we'll need to add an object that keeps track of the current game state (LOADING, LOADED, PLAYING), which is why we're also going to create a Game State object (available globally) that looks like this:

```
var GameState = {
  _current: null,
  LOADING: 0,
  LOADED: 1,
  TITLESCREEN: 2,
  PLAYING: 3
}
```

Then, depending on the current game state set in GameState._current, some objects and events are going to behave differently. For example, clicking on the title screen when the GameState._current is set to GameState.LOADING shouldn't trigger any events. However, if the GameState._current is set to GameState.TITLESCREEN, clicking on the window should display our game.

Initially, the title screen will serve as a bumper to preload our game resources such as images or sounds in the background. To do this, we're going to use an object called ResourceLoader that will allow us to download and preload all the files before we use them.

The ResourceLoader class is defined in a very straightforward way in *resourceLoader.js*:

```
// ResourceLoader class

var ResourceType = {
  IMAGE: 0,
  SOUND: 1
}

function ResourceLoader(onPartial, onComplete) {
  this.resources = [];
  this.resourcesLoaded = 0;

  if (onPartial !== undefined && typeof(onPartial) === "function") {
    this.onPartial = onPartial;
  }

  if (onComplete !== undefined && typeof(onComplete) === "function") {
    this.onComplete = onComplete;
  }
}
```

```
ResourceLoader.prototype.addResource = function(filePath, fileType, resourceType) {
  var res = {
    filePath: filePath,
    fileType: fileType,
    resourceType: resourceType
  };

  this.resources.push(res);
}

ResourceLoader.prototype.startPreloading = function() {
  for (var i = 0, len = this.resources.length; i < len; i++) {
    switch(this.resources[i].resourceType) {
      case ResourceType.IMAGE:
        var img = new Image();
        var rl = this;

        img.src = this.resources[i].filePath;
        img.addEventListener('load', function() { rl.onResourceLoaded(); }, false);
        break;
      case ResourceType.SOUND:
        var a = new Audio();

        // Only preload sound files that we can play.
        if (a.canPlayType(this.resources[i].fileType) === "maybe" ||
          a.canPlayType(this.resources[i].fileType) === "probably") {

          a.src = this.resources[i].filePath;
          a.type = this.resources[i].fileType;

          var rl = this;
          a.addEventListener('canplaythrough', function() {
            a.removeEventListener('canplaythrough', arguments.callee, false);
            rl.onResourceLoaded();
          }, false);
        } else {
          // Can't play the sound. Assume that the resource is loaded.
          this.onResourceLoaded();
        }

        break;
    }
  }
}

ResourceLoader.prototype.onResourceLoaded = function() {
  this.resourcesLoaded++;

  if (this.onPartial != undefined) {
    this.onPartial();
  }

  if (this.resourcesLoaded == this.resources.length) {
    if (this.onComplete != undefined) {
      this.onComplete();
```

```
        }
      }

      return;
    }

    ResourceLoader.prototype.isLoadComplete = function() {
      if (this.resources.length == this.resourcesLoaded) {
        return true;
      }

      return false;
    }
```

We can use the `ResourceLoader` class in the following way:

```
    var rl = new ResourceLoader();

    rl.addResource('image1.png', null, ResourceType.IMAGE);
    rl.addResource('image2.jpg', null, ResourceType.IMAGE);
    rl.addResource('image3.gif', null, ResourceType.IMAGE);
    rl.addResource('sound.ogg', 'audio/ogg', ResourceType.SOUND);
    rl.addResource('sound.mp3', 'audio/mp3', ResourceType.SOUND);

    rl.startPreloading();
```

As soon as the `ResourceLoader` method `startPreloading()` is called, we will be getting access to two very useful properties:

`ResourceLoaderInstance.resources.length`
> Returns the amount of resources added

`ResourceLoaderInstance.resourcesLoaded`
> Keeps track of how many of the resources have been preloaded so far

By combining both variables, we can calculate at any given time the percentage of resources that have been preloaded in the following way:

```
    var percentLoaded = Math.floor((ResourceLoaderInstance.resourcesLoaded * 100) /
    ResourceLoadedInstance.resources.length);
```

Additionally, the `ResourceLoader` class allows us to define two callbacks:

`onPartial`
> Called every time that an element gets loaded

`onComplete`
> Called when all resources have been loaded

Using these callbacks, it is possible to show feedback on the current status of the loading process, as shown in Figure 5-2.

Figure 5-2. Opening screen with progress bar at bottom

The game will manage different GameStates; depending on which one is the current one, a different process will be executed. To manage the transition between game states, we're going to use a function called handleGameState() that gets executed when the document finishes loading. The function uses the GameState object shown before and looks like this:

```
function handleGameState(nextState) {
  if (nextState !== undefined) {
    GameState._current = nextState;
  }

  switch(GameState._current) {
    case GameState.LOADING:
      // ...
      break;
    case GameState.LOADED:
      // ...
      break;
    case GameState.TITLESCREEN:
      // ...
      break;
    case GameState.PLAYING:
      // ...
```

```
            break;
        default:
            // ...
            break;
    }
}
```

To change the current game state, we just specify a valid `GameState` value. For example, we could easily add a `GameState.PAUSED` state that shows a paused screen when the user presses the escape key, and when it is pressed once again calls `handleGameState(Game State.PLAYING)` to get back to the game.

In the case of the `GameState.LOADING`, we're going to call a function called `preload Resources()`, which instantiates a copy of the `ResourceLoader` object to take care of preloading all the assets that we need (such as images or sounds) to run our game. The function looks like this:

```
function preloadResources(canvas, callback) {
    var c = canvas.getContext('2d');

    var rl = new ResourceLoader(printProgressBar, callback);

    rl.addResource('../img/tile.png', null, ResourceType.IMAGE);
    rl.addResource('../img/ui-icons.png', null, ResourceType.IMAGE);
    rl.addResource('../img/spritesheet.png', null, ResourceType.IMAGE);

    rl.addResource('../sounds/title.ogg', 'audio/ogg', ResourceType.SOUND);
    rl.addResource('../sounds/title.mp3', 'audio/mp3', ResourceType.SOUND);

    rl.startPreloading();

    printProgressBar();

    function printProgressBar() {
        var percent = Math.floor((rl.resourcesLoaded * 100) / rl.resources.length);

        var cwidth = Math.floor((percent * (canvas.width - 1)) / 100);

        c.fillStyle = '#000000';
        c.fillRect(0, canvas.height - 30, canvas.width, canvas.height);

        c.fillStyle = '#FFFFFF';
        c.fillRect(1, canvas.height - 28, cwidth, canvas.height - 6);
    }
}
```

This function will also print the pretty progress bar shown Figure 5-2.

You will also notice that we're not loading *cinema.png* or *tree.png*; instead, we're loading a file called *spritesheet.png*. In order to bring down the number of requests (which is a major thing to take care of in web performance optimization), instead of loading each individual image separately, we have grouped them all in a single file that we will later combine with the `Sprite` object shown in previous sections.

The resource loader instance is also receiving a parameter called `callback`, which is nothing more than `handleGameState(GameState.LOADED)` and will help us transition to the next state when the resource loading is over.

`GameState.LOADED` will be in charge of creating a "Game" instance and will also populate the tile map matrix with the building instances that we currently own. When it finishes loading the matrix, it will automatically call `handleGameState()` again, passing along `GameState.TITLESCREEN` as the next game state.

`GameState.TITLESCREEN` will show our game's title screen (which, in our case, will be the "Tourist Resort" logo and the phrase "click or tap the screen to start the game"). At the same time, it will add a listener for a "click" that will get automatically removed once the user clicks on the screen one time. When the user clicks/taps on any part of the window, the game will perform a series of fade-ins/fade-outs to white, showing the phrase "Developed by you." Finally, when the animation is over, `handleGameState()` will be called once again using `GameState.PLAYING`, which will show the game UI, print the grid with all the buildings, and start listening for events.

When *game.php*—containing our game—is requested, the server will automatically populate the Build panel to show the available buildings for construction, specifying costs, profits generated, times, and so on. Figure 5-3 shows a screenshot.

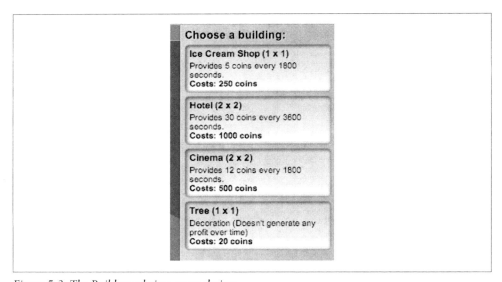

Figure 5-3. The Build panel gives users choices

Now that we're listening for input events such as scrolls, mouse up/down, key downs, and the like, in order to manage which operation a click should trigger, we're going to use an object similar to `GameState`, which keeps track of the current selected tool:

```
var Tools = {
    current: 4, // Default tool
    MOVE: 0,
    ZOOM_IN: 1,
    ZOOM_OUT: 2,
    DEMOLISH: 3,
    SELECT: 4,
    BUILD: 5
}
```

Then, when we click on the grid, the following event will be triggered and will let us handle the action appropriately:

```
Game.prototype.handleMouseDown = function(e) {
    e.preventDefault();

    switch (Tools.current) {
        case Tools.BUILD:
            // ...
            break;
        // Other tools, etc.
    }
}
```

Some actions, such as building or demolishing, also require the database fields to be updated on the server. In order to handle communications with the server, we're going to use the following functions in *comm.js*:

```
var SERVER_PATH_URL = "http://localhost:8080/";

function request(url, callback) {
    var req = false;

    if (window.XMLHttpRequest) {
        try {
            req = new XMLHttpRequest();
        } catch(e) {
            // Do nothing.
        }
    }

    if (req) {
        req.open("GET", url, true);
        req.send(null);
        req.onreadystatechange = function() {
            switch(req.readyState) {
                case 2:
                    if (req.status !== 200) {
                        callback('ERROR');
                        return;
                    }
                    break;
                case 4:
                    callback (req.responseText);
                    break;
            }
        }
```

```
      }
    } else {
      // Doesn't include support for XMLHttpRequest
      callback('ERROR');
    }
  }

  // Purchase
  function purchase(buildingId, row, col, callback) {
    var url = SERVER_PATH_URL + 'purchase.php';

    url += "?buildingId=" + buildingId;
    url += "&x=" + row;
    url += "&y=" + col;

    request(url, callback);
  }

  // Demolish
  function demolish(row, col) {
    var url = SERVER_PATH_URL + 'demolish.php';

    url += "?x=" + row;
    url += "&y=" + col;

    request(url, callback);
  }

  // Sync
  function sync() {
    var url = SERVER_PATH_URL + 'sync.php';

    request(url, callback);
  }
```

Using any of these functions is very easy. To purchase a tree (buildingId = 4) on row 4, column 5 we could use the following code:

```
purchase(4, 4, 5, function(resp) {
  if (resp.substr(0, 3) == 'OK:') {
    var buildingInstanceId = resp.substr(3, resp.length);
    alert("Building purchase was successful. The instance ID is " + buildingInstanceId);
  } else {
    alert("An error occurred while trying to purchase the building!")
  }
});
```

However, before we purchase the building, we need to check whether the clicked tile or any surrounding tiles are being occupied by another building or BuildPortion. To control this step, we're going to use a method of the Game object called Game.checkIf TileIsBusy():

```
Game.prototype.checkIfTileIsBusy = function(obj, row, col) {
  for (var i = (row + 1) - obj.tileWidth; i <= row; i++) {
    for (var j = (col + 1) - obj.tileHeight; j <= col; j++) {
```

```
        if (this.tileMap[i] != undefined && this.tileMap[i][j] != null) {
          return true;
        }
      }
    }

    return false;
}
```

Now that we have all the necessary tools to handle our events appropriately, all that we need to do to add the final implementation of the Game.prototype.handleMouse Down function:

```
Game.prototype.handleMouseDown = function(e) {
  e.preventDefault();

  switch (Tools.current) {
    case Tools.BUILD:
      if (this.buildHelper.current != null) {
        var pos = this.translatePixelsToMatrix(e.clientX, e.clientY);

        // Can we place the element on the grid?
        if (!this.checkIfTileIsBusy(this.buildHelper.current, pos.row, pos.col)) {

          var obj = this.buildHelper.current;
          var t = this;

          var processResponse = function(resp) {
            if (resp.substr(0, 3) == 'OK:') {
              var buildingInstanceId = resp.substr(3, resp.length);
              for (var i = (pos.row + 1) - obj.tileWidth; i <= pos.row; i++) {
                for (var j = (pos.col + 1) - obj.tileHeight; j <= pos.col; j++) {
                  t.tileMap[i] = (t.tileMap[i] == undefined) ? [] : t.tileMap[i];

                  t.tileMap[i][j] = (i === pos.row && j === pos.col) ? obj :
  new BuildingPortion(obj.buildingTypeId, i, j);
                }
              }
            } else {
              alert("An error occurred while trying to purchase the building!")
            }

            t.draw();
          }

          purchase(obj.buildingTypeId, pos.row, pos.col, processResponse);
        } else {
          alert("Unable purchase building on this position");
        }
      }

      break;
    case Tools.MOVE:
      this.dragHelper.active = true;
      this.dragHelper.x = e.clientX;
```

```
        this.dragHelper.y = e.clientY;
        break;
    case Tools.ZOOM_IN:
      this.zoomIn();
      break;
    case Tools.ZOOM_OUT:
      this.zoomOut();
      break;
    case Tools.DEMOLISH:

      var pos = this.translatePixelsToMatrix(e.clientX, e.clientY);

      if (this.tileMap[pos.row] != undefined && this.tileMap[pos.row][pos.col] !=
undefined) {
        var obj = this.tileMap[pos.row][pos.col];

        // Not a building, a building portion. Grab the reference to the original
building.
        if (obj instanceof BuildingPortion) {
          pos.row += obj.x;
          pos.col += obj.y;
          obj = this.tileMap[pos.row][pos.col];
        }

        var t = this;
        var processResponse = function(resp) {
          if (resp.substr(0, 2) == 'OK') {
            // Check for sorrounding pixels and destroy BuildingPortions too.
            for (var i = (pos.row + 1) - obj.tileWidth; i <= pos.row; i++) {
              for (var j = (pos.col + 1) - obj.tileHeight; j <= pos.col; j++) {
                t.tileMap[i][j] = null;
              }
            }
          } else {
            alert("A problem occurred while trying to demolish this building");
          }

          t.draw();
        }

        demolish(pos.row, pos.col, processResponse);
      }

      break;
  }

  this.draw();
}
```

Although we can now purchase or demolish buildings (adding or deleting building
instances in the database under our user), the account balance always remains the same.
In order to keep it updated, we'll implement a function called refresh() that will keep
getting called every 15 seconds, updating the account balance in the process. On the

server side, *sync.php* will also be in charge of calculating the current profits being generated by the buildings:

```
function refresh() {
  var processResponse = function(resp) {
    if (resp.substr(0, 5) == 'ERROR') {
      alert("A problem occurred while trying to sync with the service.");
    } else {
      var balanceContainer = document.getElementById('balance');

      var currBalance = parseInt(balanceContainer.innerHTML);
      var balance = parseInt(resp.substr(3, resp.length));
      balanceContainer.innerHTML = balance;
    }
  }

  sync(processResponse);
  setTimeout(function() {
    refresh(ui);
  }, 15000);
}
```

A screenshot of the game at this point can be seen in Figure 5-4.

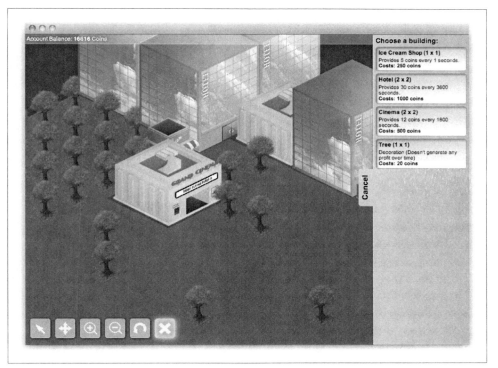

Figure 5-4. A working resort, complete with trees

Polishing the Game

The finishing touches are the things that makes a certain product (in our case, a game) feel special. Although the game so far is functional, it still feels plain, boring, and discouraging.

One method that we can use to make our game feel more alive is adding dynamic objects floating around or over the city, like clouds. Instead of using canvas to display them (which means that we would need to repaint everything every time the clouds move), we can accomplish the same effect by using CSS3 animations.

CSS3 animations allow us to modify one or multiple CSS properties over a number of keyframes in the following way:

```
@moveToRight {
  0% {
    left: 0px
  }

  50% {
    left: 100px
   }

  100% {
    left: 200px
  }
}
```

Once we have defined the animation keyframes (in this case, the element will start on position left: 0px and will move to position left: 200px), we need to define other animation properties such as:

animation-timing-function
:   Controls how each keyframe transitions to the next. Possible values are ease, linear, ease-in, ease-out, ease-in-out, cubic-bezier(*number, number, number, number*).

animation-name
:   Specifies the name of our animation (in this case, it would be moveToRight).

animation-duration
:   Controls how long the entire animation should last.

animation-iteration-count
:   Accepts either an integer value or "infinite" and controls how many times our animation should be played.

animation-direction
:   Allows us to define the "direction" of the animation. The possible values are normal (always animates from keyframe 0 to keyframe 100) or alternate (animates from keyframe 0 to keyframe 100, and then from keyframe 100 to keyframe 0).

The entire list can be found in the official W3C Working Draft at *http://www.w3.org/ TR/css3-animations/*.

Although in our case the animation will occur only in fixed positions, you can easily create the same effect using JavaScript and random variables or variables based on the current grid scroll position of our game:

```
@-webkit-keyframes moveFromLeftToRight {
  0% {
    -webkit-transform: translateX(-5000px) translateY(50px) translateZ(0px);
  }
  50% {
    -webkit-transform: translateX(0px) translateY(50px) translateZ(0px);
  }
  100% {
    -webkit-transform: translateX(5000px) translateY(50px) translateZ(0px);
  }
}

@-moz-keyframes moveFromLeftToRight {
  0% {
    -moz-transform: translateX(-5000px) translateY(50px);
  }
  50% {
    -moz-transform: translateX(0px) translateY(50px);
  }
  100% {
    -moz-transform: translateX(5000px) translateY(50px);
  }
}

@-ms-keyframes moveFromLeftToRight {
  0% {
    -ms-transform: translateX(-5000px) translateY(50px);
  }
  50% {
    -ms-transform: translateX(0px) translateY(50px);
  }
  100% {
    -ms-transform: translateX(5000px) translateY(50px);
  }
}

@-o-keyframes moveFromLeftToRight {
  0% {
    -o-transform: translateX(-5000px) translateY(50px);
  }
  50% {
    -o-transform: translateX(0px) translateY(50px);
  }
  100% {
    -o-transform: translateX(5000px) translateY(50px);
  }
}
```

```
@keyframes moveFromLeftToRight {
  0% {
    transform: translateX(-5000px) translateY(50px);
  }
  50% {
    transform: translateX(0px) translateY(50px);
  }
  100% {
    transform: translateX(5000px) translateY(50px);
  }
}

div.cloud {
  position: absolute;
  top: 0px;
  left: 0px;
  z-index: 500;
  background: transparent url(../../img/spritesheet.png) no-repeat -10px -257px;
  width: 566px;
  height: 243px;

  pointer-events: none;

  -webkit-animation-timing-function: linear;
  -webkit-animation-name: moveFromLeftToRight;
  -webkit-animation-duration: 2s;
  -webkit-animation-iteration-count: infinite;
  -webkit-animation-direction: alternate;

  -moz-animation-timing-function: linear;
  -moz-animation-name: moveFromLeftToRight;
  -moz-animation-duration: 60s;
  -moz-animation-iteration-count: infinite;
  -moz-animation-direction: alternate;

  -ms-animation-timing-function: linear;
  -ms-animation-name: moveFromLeftToRight;
  -ms-animation-duration: 60s;
  -ms-animation-iteration-count: infinite;
  -ms-animation-direction: alternate;

  -o-animation-timing-function: linear;
  -o-animation-name: moveFromLeftToRight;
  -o-animation-duration: 60s;
  -o-animation-iteration-count: infinite;
  -o-animation-direction: alternate;

  animation-timing-function: linear;
  animation-name: moveFromLeftToRight;
  animation-duration: 60s;
  animation-iteration-count: infinite;
  animation-direction: alternate;
}
```

This produces a result similar to Figure 5-5.

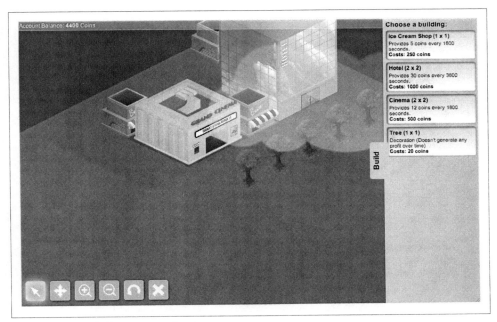

Figure 5-5. Clouds floating over the city

Another pleasant effect that would help make the scene more credible is the addition of shadows. There are several techniques and algorithms to project shadows in a two-dimensional plane; however, in most cases they need one or multiple light sources, which also requires us to perform multiple calculations, especially if we have multiple objects (which we do).

Because the objects on the scene will be static most of the time, we could efficiently either:

- Draw a shadow texture for each individual building
- Generate the shadow ourselves, dynamically

In this case, we're going to use the second approach, as it gives us the possibility of defining a pseudo-light source or controlling the intensity of the shadow dynamically.

This method consists of drawing a silhouette of the original building, then skewing and rotating it while at the same time reducing the alpha value. For example, if we painted our textures with light coming from the southeast, the shadow should be projected to the northwest. If we painted them with a light source coming from the southwest, the shadow would be projected to the northeast, and so on. Figure 5-6 will give you a better idea of what we're trying to do.

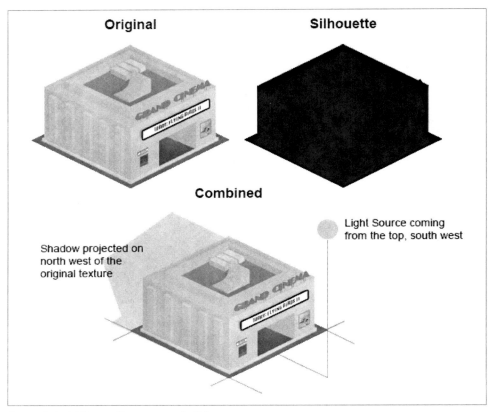

Original

Silhouette

Combined

Shadow projected on
north west of the
original texture

Light Source coming
from the top, south west

Figure 5-6. Adding a silhouette to a building

To implement this approach, we're going to resort to two HTML5 Canvas functions seen before, getImageData() and putImageData(), and we're going to build the functionality directly into the sprite object.

First, we will modify our Sprite class and add an empty property:

```
this.shadow = null;
```

Next, modify the draw() method to optionally accept a drawShadow parameter, a boolean indicating whether we want to draw a shadow to the sprite that we're drawing. A subroutine will check whether this.shadow is null and do all the necessary processing to convert the image to an image array that we can later use by calling putImage Data(). The result of the silhouette effect will be stored in our this.shadow property so that the next time that we need to use it we don't need to do all the image preprocessing again. Be advised though, that this method is less efficient than using a premade image like our shadow; however, it gives us greater control and flexibility:

```
if (this.shown) {
  if (drawShadow !== undefined && drawShadow) {
    if (this.shadow === null) { // Shadow not created yet
      var sCnv = document.createElement("canvas");
      var sCtx = sCnv.getContext("2d");

      sCnv.width = this.width;
      sCnv.height = this.height;

      sCtx.drawImage(this.spritesheet,
        this.offsetX,
        this.offsetY,
        this.width,
        this.height,
        0,
        0,
        this.width * this.zoomLevel,
        this.height * this.zoomLevel);

      var idata = sCtx.getImageData(0, 0, sCnv.width, sCnv.height);

      for (var i = 0, len = idata.data.length; i < len; i += 4) {
        idata.data[i] = 0; // R
        idata.data[i + 1] = 0; // G
        idata.data[i + 2] = 0; // B
      }

      sCtx.clearRect(0, 0, sCnv.width, sCnv.height);
      sCtx.putImageData(idata, 0, 0);

      this.shadow = sCtx;
    }

    c.save();
    c.globalAlpha = 0.1;
    var sw = this.width * this.zoomLevel;
    var sh = this.height * this.zoomLevel;
    c.drawImage(this.shadow.canvas, this.posX, this.posY - sh, sw, sh * 2);
    c.restore();
  }

  c.drawImage(this.spritesheet,
    this.offsetX,
    this.offsetY,
    this.width,
    this.height,
    this.posX,
    this.posY,
    this.width * this.zoomLevel,
    this.height * this.zoomLevel);
}
```

The end result looks like Figure 5-7.

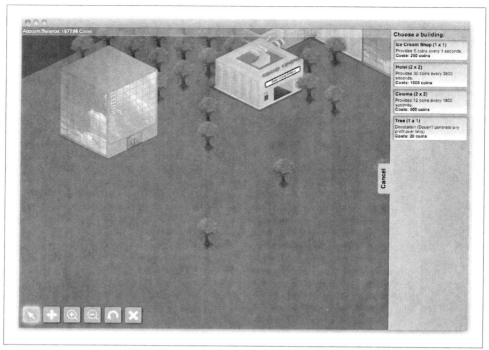

Figure 5-7. Trees with shadows

Adding a Social Networking Layer Using Facebook

Adding a social layer to our game using Facebook can be done easily by filling out some forms and implementing just a few lines of code. First, we'll need to create a new Facebook application by going to *http://www.facebook.com/developers/* and clicking on the Create New App button, which takes you to a Facebook Application Creation wizard that will allow us to integrate our game with Facebook.

Once you click the Create New App button, you'll see something like Figure 5-8 asking you to name your app.

Just type any name you want (which will be the application title seen by your users when they install the game), agree to the Terms of Service and click Create App. I named mine Tourist Resort. This name doesn't have to be unique, so feel free to name your game Tourist Resort as well.

Figure 5-8. Creating an application in Facebook

The next step, shown in Figure 5-9, is a security check that will ask you to type the text inside the captcha.

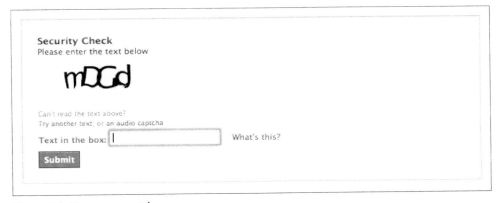

Figure 5-9. Next step: captcha

When you click Submit, depending on your account information and/or location, Facebook may ask you to verify your account by associating your telephone number or a valid credit card registered to your name.

Once you've completed these steps, you will be taken to your application management page, which will let you modify your contact information, application name and description, logo, and language, among other details.

We can integrate our application into the Facebook platform by presenting it either within the Facebook page or as a standalone application that uses Facebook's authentication scheme, called Facebook Connect. Discussing all the different Facebook authentication schemes are outside the scope of this book, so we will focus on how to display the game *within* the Facebook site.

In order to provide an external site with the logged-in user's authentication details, Facebook uses a concept called a canvas—*not* related to the HTML5 Canvas—which is nothing more than a 765-pixel-wide HTML `iframe` that loads our own site, passing along several parameters to allow us to initiate a OAuth 2.0 authentication scheme that can be done either on the server side or the client side (using JavaScript and XBFML).

> This book focuses on implementing the server-side approach. For more information on the different authentication schemes supported by the Facebook platform, please refer to *http://developers.facebook.com/docs/authentication/*.

To implement the server-side authentication scheme we're using for our game, we need to click on the Facebook Integration link on the left of our application management page. The first panel, Core Settings, shows the information in Figure 5-10.

Figure 5-10. Key information for your apps

Take note of your specific Application ID and the Application Secret (partially obscured in the figure) and download Facebook's official PHP SDK: *https://github.com/facebook/php-sdk/*.

Inside the Facebook Integration tab, we must specify two additional fields:

- The *Canvas Page*, which is a Facebook-hosted URL that will be accessed by our users when they click on our application
- The *Canvas URL*, which is the URL hosting our application

An example is shown in Figure 5-11.

Figure 5-11. Defining your canvas

In a nutshell, when users access *http://apps.facebook.com/tourist-resort*, Facebook will automatically call our Canvas URL, passing some parameters to help with the authentication.

Then, we just need to include the Facebook API files, make a new instance of the Facebook object using our Application ID and Application Secret, and we'll get access to the user's information:

```php
<?php
    require 'facebook/src/facebook.php';

    $fb = new Facebook(array(
            'appId'  => '<YOUR_APPLICATION_ID>',
            'secret' => '<YOUR_APPLICATION_SECRET>',
    ));


    $user = $fb->getUser();

    echo '<pre>';
    print_r($user);
    echo '</pre>';
?>
```

If the user is not logged in to Facebook or hasn't authorized our application yet, the output of the $user variable will be zero. A more reliable method to detect this occurrence is to use the approach taken in *example.php*, which is included in the Facebook PHP SDK:

```php
<?php
if ($user) {
    try {
            $user_profile = $fb->api('/me');
    } catch (FacebookApiException $e) {
            $user = null;
    }
}
?>
```

$fb->api('/me') tries to fill the $user_profile variable by querying Facebook's Graph API for your own user (for more information about the Facebook Graph API, see *http://developers.facebook.com/docs/reference/api/*) and throws an exception if an error occurs.

In order to let the user sign in to our application using her Facebook credentials, add the following lines:

```php
<?php
$loginUrl = $fb->getLoginUrl();
?>
<a href="<?=$loginUrl?>">Sign In</a>
```

When the user clicks Sign In, Facebook will show the authorization dialog in Figure 5-12.

Figure 5-12. Will the user grant permission?

Once the user decides to allow our application to access her data, the page will be reloaded; this time, the $user variable will be filled with the Facebook User ID and the $user_profile variable will be filled with the response to the Graph API query /me, which is returned as a JSON object.

By default, Facebook will ask for only the "basic user information," which includes things such as the user's name, last name, Facebook User ID, location, interests, gender, and so on. If we want to ask for additional permissions—for example, to get access to his email address and friends, and to be able to publish messages on his activity stream —we need to modify the $fb->getLoginUrl() call in the following way:

```php
<?php
$loginUrl = $fb->getLoginUrl(array(
    "scope" => "email, publish_stream, friends_about_me"
));
?>
```

 The entire list of permissions can be found at the following URL: *http: //developers.facebook.com/docs/authentication/permissions/*.

After we modify the permissions, our new authorization window will look like Figure 5-13.

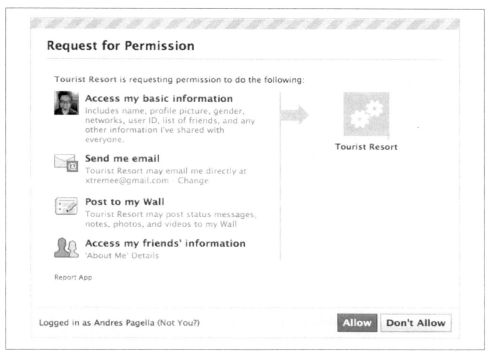

Figure 5-13. Will the user grant even more permissions?

If the user decides to allow our game to access their data, the `$user_profile` variable will include an email parameter that we can use to automatically register the user in our own database.

Once we have all the information, we can simply do a one-to-one map of the Facebook User ID with a user ID in our game to log the user in automatically when he or she connects via Facebook.

For more information, refer to the Facebook Developer website: *http://developers.face book.com/docs/guides/canvas/*.

About the Author

Andrés Pagella is an accomplished software developer with more than 10 years of professional experience, and lives in Capital Federal, Argentina. He has worked on the design and the implementation of several high-traffic websites in Argentina. He currently works as the Chief Technical Officer of Minor Studios Argentina S.R.L., developing a social game design tool called Atmosphir.

Get even more for your money.

Join the O'Reilly Community, and register the O'Reilly books you own. It's free, and you'll get:

- $4.99 ebook upgrade offer
- 40% upgrade offer on O'Reilly print books
- Membership discounts on books and events
- Free lifetime updates to ebooks and videos
- Multiple ebook formats, DRM FREE
- Participation in the O'Reilly community
- Newsletters
- Account management
- 100% Satisfaction Guarantee

Signing up is easy:

1. Go to: oreilly.com/go/register
2. Create an O'Reilly login.
3. Provide your address.
4. Register your books.

Note: English-language books only

To order books online:
oreilly.com/store

For questions about products or an order:
orders@oreilly.com

To sign up to get topic-specific email announcements and/or news about upcoming books, conferences, special offers, and new technologies:
elists@oreilly.com

For technical questions about book content:
booktech@oreilly.com

To submit new book proposals to our editors:
proposals@oreilly.com

O'Reilly books are available in multiple DRM-free ebook formats. For more information:
oreilly.com/ebooks

O'REILLY®

Spreading the knowledge of innovators   oreilly.com

The information you need, when and where you need it.

With Safari Books Online, you can:

Access the contents of thousands of technology and business books

- Quickly search over 7000 books and certification guides
- Download whole books or chapters in PDF format, at no extra cost, to print or read on the go
- Copy and paste code
- Save up to 35% on O'Reilly print books
- **New!** Access mobile-friendly books directly from cell phones and mobile devices

Stay up-to-date on emerging topics before the books are published

- Get on-demand access to evolving manuscripts.
- Interact directly with authors of upcoming books

Explore thousands of hours of video on technology and design topics

- Learn from expert video tutorials
- Watch and replay recorded conference sessions